"*Tree Stories* is a wondrous c⟨...⟩ and
poems by both adult and chi⟨...⟩ ⟨t⟩ree
that influenced the writer's l⟨...⟩ ⟨m⟩ost
delight

⟨Mid⟩west Book Review

"*Tree Stories* delights the heart with sweet songs inspired by the courage to keep still and encounter an exotic moment. *Tree Stories* takes root in the interconnectedness of all living things and will take root in your soul."
—REDWOOD MARY, *Plight of the Redwoods*

"Thank you for *Tree Stories*, and your powerful advocacy for trees. It is an extraordinary publication, one that no doubt will inspire many."
—WILLIAM H. MEADOWS, President, *The Wilderness Society*

"As *Tree Stories: A Collection of Extraordinary Encounters* so beautifully illustrates, there has long been a connection between humanity and trees. *Tree Stories* illuminates this relationship through vivid personal examples, with fine detail and a great truthfulness of expression.
—JOHN ROSENOW, President, *The National Arbor Day Foundation*

"Advice from a Tree: Stand tall and proud, be flexible, remember your roots, drink plenty of water and enjoy the view! *Tree Stories* is a wonderful book."
—ILAN SHAMIR, author of *Advice from a Tree*®

TREE STORIES

*A Collection
of
Extraordinary Encounters*

Edited by
Warren David Jacobs and Karen I. Shragg

SunShine Press Publications

SunShine Press Publications, Inc.
P. O. Box 333
Hygiene, CO 80533
www.sunshinepress.com
sunshinepress@sunshinepress.com

Copyright © 2002 Warren David Jacobs and Karen I. Shragg

Cover design by J. Hofer
Cover photograph of Cades Cove Maple Tree by Carol Weeks

Library of Congress Cataloging-in-Publication Data

Tree stories : a collection of extraordinary encounters / edited by
Warren David Jacobs and Karen I. Shragg

p. cm.

ISBN: 1-888604-22-0

1. Trees--United States--Anecdotes. 2. Trees--Poetry. I. Jacobs,
Warren David, 1943-   II. Shragg, Karen, 1954-

QK115.T74 2002
810.8'0364--dc21

2001057626

Printed in the United States
5 4 3 2
Printed on recycled acid-free paper using soy ink

Table of Contents

Foreword

One of my most vivid childhood memories is of standing in our front yard in Tupelo, Mississippi, looking up at a big oak tree and trying to figure out how in the world I was going to climb it. Lots of young boys begin their relationships with trees that way. In the tenth grade, my affection for trees deepened as I worked on a major tree-and-leaf project for my biology class. Fortunately, Rhodes College in Memphis, where we had moved, had a wonderful arboretum, with hundreds of trees identified. I spent hour after fascinating hour with those great trees.

Years later, while living in California, I had the opportunity to see trees I had only read about. It is truly humbling to stand amidst Giant Sequoia and Redwoods, and I was grateful that our forebears had realized the importance of saving some of them. Another high point was a visit to Cedar Breaks National Monument in Utah, where I saw my first bristlecone pine trees, the Earth's oldest living inhabitants.

Sometimes we get so caught up in the beauty of trees and their emotional tugs on us that we lose sight of all the things they do to make our lives better. They clean the air, filter our water and provide wildlife with food and shelter, to name just three benefits.

Of course, it is the comfort, inspiration or excitement provided by trees that really grabs us. Whether it's the flowering dogwood out back or the towering Sitka spruce in Alaska's Tongass National Forest, trees have always been special to people. As we become more urban, their importance becomes even greater. I can think of almost nothing more peaceful than stretching out in a grove of trees on a hot summer day and just listening to the sounds of nature—or reading a book like *Tree Stories*.

William H. Meadows
President, The Wilderness Society
March 13, 2003

Preface

In 1971, while on a life-altering move from Chicago to Columbus, Georgia, I met and fell in love with a maple tree in Cades Cove, a magnificently beautiful area in the Great Smoky Mountains National Park. She became an integral part of my life, and over the next eighteen years, I visited her often, in times of joy and pain, continually receiving nurturing, spiritual enrichment, and healing wisdom. I was certain that I would forever be able to sit under her canopy.

After a hiatus of seven years, I returned to my maple in October, 1996, only to find, to my horror, that she had died, having been struck by lightning in 1994. Thus began my journey, which has culminated with the creation of this anthology.

Following my heartrending discovery, I spoke with several officials of the Park Service, attempting to convince them of the importance of planting another tree where mine had stood—a fitting, healing memorial to her life. The people with whom I spoke were very cordial and caring, but Park regulations and other under-standable considerations made my wish an impossibility. Through discussions with local residents, I discovered that other individuals also loved this tree and that she was called "The Wedding Tree," as many couples chose to be married under her watchful protection. I then entertained the desire to convene a meeting of "lovers of the Cades Cove maple tree," where we would share stories of our connections with her. I even managed to negotiate an interview with a reporter for the local Gatlinburg, Tennessee, newspaper to publicize my idea, but, sadly, I received only a few responses. I'm not certain, but perhaps the title of the front-page article, 'Psychiatrist Seeks Tree Stories,' influenced the response!

I was quite disappointed until I realized that I could expand my idea for a memorial to my tree and create a collection of stories from people who have had meaningful encounters with "their" tree(s). And as I began to ask relatives, friends, and acquaintances for their submissions, it was my great fortune to meet Karen Ilene

Shragg. My daughter, Elana, spoke with Karen about my project, and with her characteristically infectious enthusiasm and positive, loving energy, Karen volunteered to help. I am truly blessed and deeply grateful for her friendship, dedication, creativity, and wisdom.

Regarding my own connection with trees, I must admit to being a "late bloomer." Having spent my childhood in the inner city ghetto of the old Jewish West Side of Chicago, I was not particularly cognizant of the existence of trees. I don't recall having been drawn to tree climbing (good Jewish boys didn't do such things), I had no access to tree swings, and my connection to them was relegated to the distant appreciation of their beauty. In early adolescence, my family moved to a house in the suburbs, where my father planted several trees in our backyard. But other than enjoying the summer shade, I felt no special bond with them.

When I was seventeen I spent a year in Israel, and I began to understand the wonder of nature, the importance of trees, and the Hand of God. While studying in a youth leadership course, I learned that trees were vital to Israel's security by providing barriers of protection from the surrounding hostile nations, that forests helped to stabilize the land from the ravages of erosion, that trees had reclaimed the desert. I learned that one could plant a tree to celebrate a joyous occasion—a birth, a Bar/Bat Mitzvah, a wedding, an anniversary. And I learned that trees were living memorials to individuals and to the countless millions who were slaughtered during the Holocaust.

The Jewish tradition evidences great respect and reverence for trees (the Tree of Life, the Tree of Knowledge of Good and Evil, and the *Torah*—Five Books of Moses—is likened to a tree), other world traditions appreciate their deep spiritual energy, and I have grown to understand and value my personal relationship with one of nature's oldest living beings.

It is my fervent hope that you, the reader of these wonderfully moving and enriching stories and poems, will be touched in your heart and soul, and that you will awaken to the sacred kinship we all have with trees and to the Unity of All.

—*Warren David Jacobs*

Introduction

There is a concept represented by the Yiddish word "Bashert" that relates to the beginning of how this book got started. Bashert means that sometimes bad things happen that later take on a positive spin, even if that silver lining is not clear at first. Warren had a tree that came into his life as an adult. It was the death of that tree and the subsequent feelings of grief that sent him looking for others who might have a similar story. I found his story so compelling that I volunteered to become his partner in the quest to seek out others who had a tree story. Of course, I found it to be such a wonderful idea because I, too, had a special tree in my life, one that I connected strongly with during my elementary school years.

In the process of searching for these stories, we found that just by asking to listen to the private connections people had to a tree, we unleashed profound feelings in the authors. Universally, they thanked us for allowing them the opportunity to tell their stories. Somehow, these trees had shaped their lives yet it seemed silly to tell their stories in any social context. *Tree Stories* provided them with the proper medium in which to bare their soul about their special tree. It became clear to me, during the collection of these personal stories and poems, that the reason there is no social context for sharing them is that our modern day culture does little to encourage these connections. On the contrary, it is considered a bit bizarre to have a meaningful relationship with an "inanimate" object. Although science can prove that trees are living, breathing organisms, we have been told all our lives to look at trees as things to be used for everything from housing materials to paper. How convenient for the industries that rely on our purchases of products made from trees!

In contrast, indigenous cultures promote relationships with trees and animals as a part of daily life. Having a relationship with a tree is seen as normal in their societies as it is to have microwave ovens in ours. That is why it is so astounding to find the storytellers in this book, and the many others, who still have stories to tell. Somehow the various trees in the following stories added a dimension to the authors' lives that changed them for the better. One doesn't need to take a formal survey to realize that the opportunities for people to connect with trees today are very diminished. Life is less rural; it is less safe to play in trees without thinking about lawsuits and medical costs. Urban children's feet barely touch anything but pavement, let alone have trees to safely climb. These stories may represent a time that is sadly just about over, a time when trees and people spent more time together. Or, perhaps this is the beginning of a new paradigm which provides for a balance between people and green spaces. A time when our lives are enriched as we embrace all life forms and come to see ourselves as a part of this whole spectacular planet.

—Karen I. Shragg

Think Like a Tree
by Karen I. Shragg

Soak up the sun
Affirm life's magic
Be graceful in the wind
Stand tall after a storm
Feel refreshed after it rains
Grow strong without notice
Be prepared for each season
Provide shelter to strangers
Hang tough through a cold spell
Emerge renewed at the first signs of spring
Stay deeply rooted while reaching for the sky
Be still long enough to
hear your own leaves rustling.

Chapter One

Trees as Teachers

There is a tree by the river and we have been watching it day after day for several weeks when the sun is about to rise.... As you sit there, there is a relationship of deep abiding security and a freedom that only trees can know.... If you establish a relationship with it, then you have relationship with mankind. You are responsible then for that tree and for the trees of the world. But if you have no relationship with the living things on this earth, you may lose whatever relationship you have with humanity, with human beings.

—*J. Krishnamurti*

The Loving of Trees
by C. B. Follett

I am in love with trees
I know it sounds daft
but I can't help it.

I love the stability of them
their to and sway.

I love their general health
the outward persona
that keeps council of inner griefs.

I like how they resist the crack
of winds, the bleach of sun.

Even blighted ponderosa
and beetled lodgepole
where the sap comes out red and cruciform
instead of honeyed taffy, even then
as bells toll in browned needles
they retain an erect dignity.

I want to hold them
tell them my regret at drinking
their birthright, at fouling the air
we share, breaking their resistance.

They don't seem to ask this of me
stand noble as kings along the ridge
branches touching or not
birds coming or not.

I love them for their stance
and for never forgetting
to reach upward.

Scar Tree
by Shanti Benoit

Morning is my time to walk in the woods. Early, while dew still sparkles from Spanish moss and spider web. When ferns are green as emerald and red manzanita dark as blood in the saturated light of dawn. Clues to the unfolding mystery of each new day.

A Redwood tree stands beside my trail. At one time a fire swept through this part of the forest. I believe the reason this Redwood still stands (it's the only old growth left) is that it burned on one side almost to the top and down to its core, useless for logging. But the giant didn't die. It grew around its wound and flourished.

I have a scar on the trunk of my body as a result of surgery when I was twenty. The tree has become a totem of survival for me. I bring it offerings. I bring roses from my garden, placing the yellow, white, pink and red blossoms into the charred, cracked wood. I sit beneath it, pray for healing, and make intentions for my life. I embrace it. We talk.

One morning, after walking through fern and manzanita down the hill to the tree, I find a Raven feather placed next to my Fire Princess rose. This excites me. Perhaps it's a communication. But from whom?

The next morning I pick a Cecil Brunner bud from my garden fence and insert it beside the blue-black feather. Days go by with no response. When I'm about to give up, a Hawk feather appears. I now believe it's intentional and I fantasize. I imagine a friend who knows about the tree, placing it there to mystify me. I imagine a wood spirit answering a prayer. I secretly dream of a wise man, a man with a soul who understands the language of roses and feathers, knows the healing power of the forest.

I imagine the two of us on the forest floor covered in leaves and twigs as we embrace unseen in the root arms of the trees, so blended with the pulse of nature that we only cause a slight stir among the ferns.

I answer the Hawk feather with a New Dawn rose delicate with paper thin petals and a bright yellow center. Again, days go by with no response. Then, another feather appears. A yellow and black Tanager feather smooth as satin. The next day I tender one of my Peace roses, fully opened, but it looks ostentatious next to the other offerings. I want to make a grandiose statement but fear I say too much, too soon. I hurry back with a smaller Jacob's Coat, flame petals of crimson and yellow. The Jacob's Coat is answered with the salmon feather of a Flicker. I am gratified that the response comes so soon, and wanting to keep the conversation going, I fix a sprig of old-fashioned Blaze roses into a charred crack in the tree's center. I place a polished river stone beside them.

In the morning I find a sea shell. My excitement intensifies. The following day I race back with a small spray of Glowing Embers, soft as love.

A week passes with no answer. Not feather, shell, nor stone. My disappointment can't be measured. Then I have a haunting dream.

I hold a door closed to a tremendous dark force. Fire serpents push at me from the other side. When I feel I can hold no longer, Feather person is there. I can't see the face, but the figure, close behind me, helps hold the frightful door and together we keep the monster at bay. Then our strength begins to fail. I can feel arms on either side of me, embracing me. I can feel them grow thin and begin to weaken. I hear a whisper in my ear, then, "We must let go!" And we do. We are pulled into a vortex spinning down and down. I am held in skeleton arms as we whirl into ecstatic oblivion.

My desire to know Feather person intensifies. I am deep in love with an imagined being. I change my routine, visit the woods in the afternoon, hoping to meet this unknown person. I see two jogging women plugged into Walkmans, a group of children on bicycles, and a man with a cane walking a dog. They all pass the tree without awareness.

I decide to pack my lunch and wait. I find a spot off the path opposite the tree. On the third afternoon, settled in, hidden well in a thicket, I hear someone. Footsteps make a hollow crunch on the woodland duff. I crouch down as far as I can. A man is coming; I can see him clearly now. His clothes are shabby and filthy, his hair unwashed and in sad dreadlocks. His torn shoes are held together with duct tape. His face is ageless—ravaged and thin. The veil of skin over his bones fine, almost translucent. My stomach goes hollow and my heart turns fist, pounding my chest.

The man leans into the tree on a bone-thin arm. He reaches into a dirty backpack, removes a White Owl feather, and places it beside my Glowing Embers.

I can't believe what I see. He is a bum. Sickly and disgusting. What could I do? How could I get away? My romantic fantasies fall into dust and I lie silent on the forest floor. I hold my breath and shield my eyes. If I can't see him, he won't exist. But he soon shuffles off without looking back. And I'm glad he's gone. I communicated by feather and rose with this vagabond. Disfigured. Scarred.

My spiteful words echo in my ears. He is scarred, scarred, yes like the tree and scarred like me!

In the introspection of the days that follow, I know I must keep the connection alive. After all, we are all woven into the web of life no matter how difficult or unfortunate our lives might be. So I not only bring roses for Feather man, I offer food wrapped in foil which I tuck into the folds of the tree and raid the thrift store for a warm hat and coat. Each time I return my offerings are gone. At times I find a feather or stone.

One early morning, before the sun tops the trees, I find yesterday's food where I left it. Untouched, untaken. I persist with my offering of food and clothing but each day I find them, unclaimed. The Feather man is gone. I spend afternoons as before, in my hiding place, hoping to catch sight of him, but he has vanished.

A few weeks later I pick up a local newspaper and find a story about a man found dead near the river. A homeless man found by loggers. No one knows his name or where he comes from. They found his body at a small encampment hidden in the woods. It is reported that he lived there for some time. I want to tell them he has an identity. He is Feather man! But what would be the use? I imagine the camp being cleaned by foresters placing his meager belongings into black plastic bags with the last roses I brought, a branch of apple blossom scented Dream Weavers.

I ask the tree why we lost him. Silence. The tree stands unchanged by the passing of this man. I stretch my arms upward, stand straight and silent. I want to be like the tree. I listen to the branches stirring in the wind. I watch them nod in affirmation. There is a whisper. A whisper that sings of survival. The voice enfolds me, gives me comfort. For in that moment, without a doubt,

I know that this man is a soul, and however lost in his body, he is now spinning into realms of possibility leaving feathers to mark the way.

The Willow Tree
by Jill Hammer

Elat Chayyim, a retreat center in Accord, New York, is a place for Jews who are looking for ways to renew Judaism. In any given week of the summer, there are several prayer groups there. I found my place in the "traditional" prayer group, an egalitarian service which that week was led by Michael Lerner and Reb Zalman Schachter-Shalomi. It was there that I came across an extraordinary willow tree.

In the traditional Jewish morning service, called *Shacharit,* dawning, there is a blessing over the light of creation. In an unusual move, the fifteen or so of us walked out through the white-trimmed door of the red barn, which was our synagogue, and down its wooden steps to feel creation firsthand. Our feet brushed the grass and our eyes were bathed in sunlight. Sighing with pleasure, each of us found a spot where we felt ready to go on with the prayers.

In the Jewish tradition, *makom kavua,* fixed place, is an important concept. One is expected to establish a place of prayer where one feels comfortable: a certain bench, a back row seat, a corner of one's home. That morning, in new surroundings, I took my stand beside a large willow. The green-gold branches dipped down like braids. The group continued along the flow of ancient words, and I began to feel the tree as a distinct presence, praising God with us in its own rustling way.

When the rest of the group filed back inside to continue the service, I stayed at my place, wanting to focus myself on creation as I prayed. Out of the corner of my eye, I saw a young man delightedly stroke the bark of a gnarled vine as he climbed the steps of the barn. I was moved by his gesture. As I began the *Amidah,* the silent, standing prayer which is the focus of Jewish worship, I reached out my hand and took a branch of the willow tree in my fingers.

The branch felt soft, complex and gentle. I felt as if I were holding the hand of an older sister, one who knew much more than

I did about the ways of the world, and was willing to teach me. The willow tree rooted me and grounded me, although it swayed and bowed just as I did. It seemed to have its own order of worship, one even more ancient than my own, and suddenly I was curious about the praise offered by trees. The willow lent me its wordless guidance willingly. In Jewish lore the willow symbolizes humility, and that day I learned a lesson in humble acceptance of the universe and its creatures. As small as I was, I felt perfectly loved. When the time came, I did not want to let go my fistful of leaves.

When I returned to Elat Chayyim two years later, the willow's branches were being trimmed by noisy machines. I could no longer reach the handlike green-gold twigs, but I looked up at the tree with fondness. That year I was the one who led services. I like to think I learned something about prayer from my sister the willow tree.

Cultivating Knowledge
by Richard Beban

As a child, I loved grandfather's
fruit trees, drunk with blossoms
& smelling of strange yellow sap.
Loved them for transporting me
above my young condition
for a moment taller than he,
I could see beyond
the fence to the mysteries
of other people's yards.

I loved them for exploding sweet
fresh apricots, yellow furry skins pneumatic
& bursting. Or green apple crackling
in the mouth, sometimes loosening a tooth
that overnight became a shiny dime.

For the joy they gave him
in grafting. Take two strains,
cut across the rough bark
at a sharp angle, press them together
with care & coiled brown string,
salve the wound with pitch
& someday they yield a hybrid—
a third life bursting forth after the proper
quickening, a season or two
that seemed like forever.

I learned from his trees how learning is born:
Take a fact, cut across at a sharp angle,
match with a second fact, bind them with
some mystery glimpsed at a distance,
no salve is needed. New life bathes
brain cells in joy as tasty as juice
from grandfather's finest Rome Beauties.

Carrying Water to Trees
by Louis Martinelli

I have lived in three farmhouses in my life—two of them more or less New England saltbox in design and one a wood frame house built up around what was originally a log cabin. The logs were discovered when the owner of the house tore out the interior of the kitchen to build a chimney for a wood burning stove.

The logs were maple, a fairly common tree used to build houses before 1940, and they were two feet in diameter. The chimney builder ruined two saws trying to cut through the logs, and one of his co-workers accidentally dropped a third saw from the roof, breaking a window.

One of the conditions for my living in the maple log house was that I act as a gatekeeper for the owner. That meant I would wear various hats at various times, depending on who threatened the land with damage. Since game was plentiful there, especially trophy-sized deer and a growing population of pheasants, one of my duties was to walk the fence lines and see that they were not transgressed. Another was to keep a road open from the house to the main highway, and then again from the house to the river which bordered the property. Windfalls after storms were the primary obstacles to be removed. I got to know and admire the place, especially its trees, on my daily walks to the river. I got to know the river my first summer by stopping to fish it, and in the fall and early winter, by sitting on an abandoned railroad bridge and watching the stars rise and shine on the water.

More than anything, I liked discovering the trees: mature red and white cedar, juniper, several kinds of birch, red and white pine, oak and elm, shag-bark hickory, cottonwood, box elder, a few Kentucky coffee trees. None of these were old growth, but they surrounded agricultural fields, provided habitat for deer, red fox, ring-necked pheasant, ruffed grouse, a covey of quail and a large number of song birds. They provided a windbreak in the winter for the fields and the house, and shade in the summer. They were thick and beautiful to look at: a small oasis of forest in the middle of largely overplowed agricultural land.

On one of my walks, I watched as snow fell and caught in the green branches of a common juniper. I was as transfixed by the new snow nesting in the small tree as the tree itself was enclosed by the snow it held. There was an element of worship in my feeling, as if I were witnessing revelation itself.

When I returned the next day, the snow had melted away in the morning sun. But there was imprinted in me the union of juniper and white crystal flakes of snow with the knowledge of winter's heart, to be read like a book in the common juniper.

One day my landlord announced he was going to have to cut down some trees in order to make his loan payment. He did not want to as he had promised the previous owner, an elderly woman, he would never cut down the cedar trees. But now he had to cut down some cedar and even more oak. For every tree he cut down he promised to plant a hundred saplings somewhere on the land. He would plant maple trees and oak and river birch and pine. It would be all right.

The cedar and oak trees were cut in the late summer, before an unusually wet fall. Erosion followed, a hillside sagged, the logging roads developed ruts and became muddy pools of water.

A well-intentioned man, an engineer by profession, the land owner was true to his word. With the help of his sons, the new trees were planted the following spring and summer. Inspired by five majestic eastern white pines towering above the house, he planted many pines, some in unlikely places.

The summer proved to be one of the hottest and driest in memory in the upper Midwest. Drought is more than the absence of rain; it is a condition which damages anything vulnerable to it. The saplings began to show signs of extreme stress from the dry heat. Particularly hard hit were the pine, which turned brown and withered sooner than the maple, oak or birch.

I spent time each day carrying water out to the young trees in ten-gallon containers, only a few of the plantings were close enough to the house to reach with a garden hose. I was confident I could save them; so I did not ask for help. It was a noble exercise in futility. By the middle of July, two thirds of the trees were beyond recovery, and by early September, I was hard-pressed to find a dozen healthy trees.

So far as I could tell, the plantings had been done at the proper time and soil depth and everything was accounted for except the one variable least visible to us humans: our exaggerated pride. The land owner, the loggers and the planters had all failed to consider the possibility of too much rain and not enough rain occurring in the same year. I had failed to consider my own helplessness in saving the vulnerable saplings. Good intentions or noble ends cannot overcome bad or inadequate means.

The land surrounding the maple log house needed less engineering and gatekeeping and more caregiving, I think. The indiscriminate cutting became the end of the trees, the beginning of erosion, and the loss of healthy soil. Do no harm, the first principle of ethics in the practice of medicine, is equally important in the practice of land ownership.

What the earth has come to need, increasingly, is the carefulness and refusal to harm that we associate, historically, with nursing. To treat land well, or restore to health land that has been damaged, is a kind of caregiving that is primary to the healing of nature.

Waiting for a Message
by Rochelle Mass

Trees help you see slices of sky between branches,
point to things you could never reach.
Trees help you watch the growing happen,
watch blossoms burst then dry,
see shade twist to the pace of the sun,
birds tear at unwilling seeds.

Trees take the eye to where it is,
where it was,
then over to distant hills,
faraway to other places and times,
long ago.

A tree is a lens,
a viewfinder, a window.
I wait below
for a message
of what is yet to come.

Tree Epiphany
by Nicole S. Urdang

Like spilling one's guts to a stranger on a train, and never learning her name, I don't know what kind of a tree you were.

I was in Ojai, California, in December of '96 at a conference. There were many people and only one phone; so I had little contact with my family, which only added to my feeling of isolation. My friend, with whom I was rooming, had acted in ways I thought were disloyal, and I felt as if there was an emotional gulf between us as wide as Asia. I decided to re-center myself by doing a walking meditation.

I had been eyeing a multibranched, clump base tree sequestered by itself in a very inviting area, and knew that was where I wanted to walk.

Walking slowly is "de rigueur" for a meditation like this; the distance traveled is measured in the spirit/mind, not in miles, and not on terra firma.

I started pacing back and forth at the base of the tree, carefully paying attention (this was mindfulness meditation, after all) to the ground under my feet, the blue sky, the weight of each leg as it hit the ground, the branches above me, the temperature, scents, bird calls, and my breath.

Soon, I found myself profoundly calm. When I looked up at the branches, my relationship with my friend fell into place. I realized that just as those branches separate, some seeking the sun, and others reuniting and intertwining with the original one from which it split, my friend and I had psychically parted company. Whether we would reunite again was anyone's guess.

One year has passed since that day, and while I wasn't able to make the break with my friend until last month, I am once again at peace, having learned a lesson from a quiet tree in Ojai.

Tree, Why Do You Bind Me?
by Laura Snyder

I want to tell what the forests were like
I will have to speak
in a forgotten language
—W. S. Mervan

So deeply in the forest you were hidden, I almost missed you when my eyes slid past you, but I heard your call. You touched my elemental core with that one glance. For you are sheer primeval power. Calling, you demand a response, a commitment—abandon. There was an instant recognition, a knowledge that somehow we are one, bound together intimately cell to cell in age-old mysteries I never believed had merit.

Who are you that you should arrest me so completely and hold me to your vision through past ages? I was so overcome with delight at your compelling speech, I felt my only choice was to rush you, rip my clothes away and dance and dance in joy at my first sight of you. You are the tree to cause one to weep or to risk death.

You stand solid, massive in girth. Your cinnamon bark has been plowed with furrows a foot deep by the dappled light and dark of years, years and years. How have you borne the weight of all those years? Through tearing aeons of dynamic change, through all its ebb and flow, you remain a testimony of resilient tenacity.

How have you held on to this life? Your roots and needles holding earth to sky as close as an anchor through the riptides of epochs and kingdoms. Politics have swirled the earth in baths of blood, and exalted peoples have vanished into forgotten mists, yet you remain.

You were centuries old when the Renaissance transformed whole systems of thought and beliefs. You first pushed forth from your winged seed in the age of chivalry. You are old and your story would be true.

How have your cells recorded history? I want my own

visionless cells to press into the deep rifts of your corky sides to read the true lessons of history that really matter. The lines are scribed there waiting for someone of discernment to read. Although I am compelled to rush you, I draw back. How could my human frame contain the cup of life from which you have drunk? I know not what you are asking of me.

As I watch, the wind plays you and you groan, the sun warms you and you sigh. How often have you cried out in loneliness in the midst of the humble native shrubs of salal and kinnikinnick? Who is there around you old enough to understand the burden of all you have witnessed?

Who remains to listen? Do you grow weary of speaking to stones? They are the only ones old enough to remember. As I listen, I hear a river of deep speech, but I do not understand the currents.

The surrounding mixed forest of fir, hemlock and alder is young and insignificant. They are like scrub before your majesty. There is no one here left like you, no one at all.

Do you weep as you instruct the immature trees in the rhythmic cadence necessary for the deep stomatal breaths? Where stand the other ancient teachers who could carry the drumbeat strong that life should continue to have breath upon the earth? Will the young trees be sufficient to keep the beat for all the green grasses, herbs and woody shrubs when you are gone?

Finally, I ask you, why were you spared when your brethren were felled? It must have been an axeman with pegged pants and cork-soled boots who you bound in like manner with your charm. So different from me, so far removed in lifestyle, did he struggle with his feeling as I have? He must have felt as alone in his visions and calling as have I.

I applaud his sacrifice to save you. For your kindred brothers and their children were silenced in the time of his axe. The loud singing of the ancients was cut off. The reflected light from primeval faces has been replaced in this day by juvenile profiles untried by century's carvings and I, I remain bound to you searching for understanding.

My age is nothing. The significance of my accomplishments are less than the lichen's gold stain upon your bark. Why have you called me to speak? I cannot even hold back one insect blazing a

path across your vertical terrain. How can I save you? My bones
will turn to ash before your cambium lays down fifty more rings of
time. Why do you bind me, tree?

   Author's Note: This old-growth Douglas Fir is unprotected on Fox
Island in Puget Sound in the State of Washington.

How To Enjoy A Tree
by Vivina Ciolli

In every moment we are
the source of our own happiness.
—Avadhoota Da Free John

In spring, approach an old tree
with caution
while counting backward from 53.

Find each color in its bark and leaves.
Name the opposite color.

Choose a young tree.
Use a stethoscope,
and listen to its heartbeat.

Place your shoulder on a tree
about as wide around as you are.
Fling open your arms.
Hug the tree for a long time.
Press your cheek against its trunk.

This close, inhale deeply.
Hold your breath with the scent of tree.
Lick the tree's rough surface,
like a lover.

Step back. Bury your face in your hands.
Know you have been loved.

Chapter Two

Trees As Nurturers

Alone with myself
The trees bend to caress me
The shade hugs my heart.
—*Candy Polgar*

A Maple
by Michael Collins

I'm in the backyard running, playing ball. The tennis ball arcs through the afternoon sky, my eyes hawk it, fighting the sun. I'm ten, and catching tennis balls is everything in the world.

From the hedges covering a rusted chain-link fence to a maple across the yard, the ball traces the same parabolic course, over and over. With each flight I watch it creep toward its apex. Like a springboard diver or a biplane losing its engine, it levels, then falls. Its descent thrills me, my legs respond in a sharp twitch as I bound across the yard, driven by conjured desperation. Timing my sprint, I pull the green ball from my shoe-tops, tumbling forward, rolling over, the third out secured in the webbing of my glove, stopping at the foot of the maple tree. The bases were loaded. They're always loaded.

"Why do you keep doing that?"

I looked around, embarrassed that someone had been watching, angry that they had invaded my world of grass-stained catches and ninth-inning heroics. I saw no one. I looked at the maple tree.

"Don't look at me like you're surprised," the maple tree said. "You've known the whole time that I was here watching. That's why you keep on showing off. It's for me, right?"

"I wasn't showing off."

"You were showing off. You always show off. I think that you do it for me; you want me to like you."

"What are you talking about? You're a tree; I don't want you to like me."

"Yes, you do. You think I'm cute."

I turned, walking away.

"I think you're cute," she said.

A maple tree thought I was cute. I threw down my glove. I wanted to go on with the game, but now I would feel caged by the presence of the maple, my recklessness smothered, my situational dream world now vacated until I could regain confidence in my isolation. I picked up a wooden bat and walked closer to the house.

"Where are you going? I'm sorry, I only want to talk to you."

I flipped the ball up and smacked it with the bat. The ball popped up onto the roof of the house and began to skip back down, the third carom dropping it back at my feet. I picked it up and clubbed it again.

"You shouldn't feel funny talking to me. I just thought that since you spend so much time back here with me that maybe we could be friends."

The tennis ball rolled down the roof, the hops smoother this time, and stuck in the gutter. I went into the garage and dragged back a ladder, fished the ball from the stench of rotting leaves, and resumed hitting.

"Why do you practice so much? You must be terrible to need so much practice. Maybe you should just quit. It's a stupid game anyway."

My body swelled, the maple was taunting me, trying to draw me in.

"Why don't you like talking to me? You spoke to me before, you know. Do you remember two years ago when you were sick and you had to go to the hospital? You had pneumonia. You spoke to me then."

She was right. I did remember being sick and going to the hospital. And I remembered how the night before she came across the yard to my window and she stayed with me, and when she spoke to me I could feel my fever spilling away. My mother came into my room later and I told her about the maple, and what she did. In the hospital, I told the doctor. It was common, he told my mother. My fever had made me delirious. One hundred five degrees will do that to a child. That was what he said. Still, I knew what she had done and I loved her for it. Maybe that is why I had been showing off, bouncing across the lawn, carried by playschool acrobatics, sprawling in front of her, the court jester performing for a regal presence. I dropped the bat and walked over to the maple.

Standing beneath the long limbs I drew my hand over the bark. Its surface was rough, marking the soft skin of my palm with white scrapes. Searching for a heartbeat, I held my hand in place before leaping up and grabbing the lowest branch. Hanging there I was able to hook my leg over the branch and pull myself up into the maple.

"What are you doing?" she said.

"I want to see something. I want to see out of the top."

"You can't go all the way to the top. I won't be able to hold you that high."

I didn't listen to her. The branches were thick and strong; they could hold me here for eight hundred years. The maple's structure was made for my body. Grips and footholds emanated from her sweet brown skin, making the top no more than a quick scamper. The more distance I put between me and the ground, the more my confidence grew. I gained the sense that I was supposed to be here, scaling a maple, my balance and strength enhanced by my journey. My weight began to bend the smaller branches, shaking the green leaves that now hid me from view.

"You're climbing too high," the maple said to me.

"No I'm not. Besides, I'm almost there."

Crawling, I eased my body up into the thinnest groupings of branches. With my knees tucked in front of me, I remained perched on a network of thin twigs. As I looked up, a layer of leaves covered me like the skin of a bubble. To break through all I would have to do was stand up.

"Please climb back down," the maple implored. "Why won't you listen to me? There's nothing to see anyway."

"For you there's nothing, but I want to see anyway. I want to see what you see. Do you think I can stand?"

"No, but you're going to do it anyway, right?" Her voice cracked as if in tears.

Fresh growth and dead twigs both channeled out from the last thin branch directly above me. I reached up and grabbed the leaves. Then, using the leaves for balance, I began to stand. My legs began to lift me, my sneakers sensing for a weakness in my footing, the branches swaying, bending like the arm of a bow. My head began to pass through the crown of the maple. Her green leaves felt cool against my face, the smell of new growth rubbing off onto my clothes, permeating my lungs. Clearing her crown, I penetrated into sunlight.

My eyes carried across everything I knew. Colored shingles of neighborhood rooftops, my school and playground, even the train station, the people dressed in their summer colors, flecked along the platform, a smattering of colored sprinkles. Everything laid out in front of me like one of my board games. I turned my head and found the food store that my mother went to, and far behind it I saw the smokestack of the factory where my father worked.

I twisted my neck further, trying to turn my head without moving my body. Another breeze moved through the top of the maple, and a gentle rocking stirred through the crown. I squeezed the leaves tighter in an attempt to steady my footing and to slow the bobbing of my head which had slipped into the rhythm of the swirling foliage. The only sight I did not seem to be looking down upon was the cathedral. Its steep roof narrowed with its ascent, filing to a point, supporting the cross balanced at its apex. Beyond the cathedral, almost too far to distinguish, were the black spikes of the wrought iron fence surrounding the cemetery.

Again the maple swayed from a strong breeze. The wind was sustained this time, and my grip on the leaves became strained. Shuffling my feet, I tried to regain my delicate perch, but the rocking escalated. In wild undulations, the maple whirled around me in sweeping motions, the sounds of twigs brushing with leaves storming my senses, the branch beneath me straining with my weight, then giving way. I reached out but the tiny dead branches I grabbed gave way like morning icicles, crumbling in my hands. I dropped to a lower branch but the force of my body snapped it away, its jagged end ripping my shorts and piercing my leg. For one violent instant my body jerked to a stop. Screaming, I pushed away from the impaling as the line of my free fall continued. In streaks and flashes the maple blurred by. My speed increased, tears were pulled from my eyes, and as I closed the distance to the ground the maple lurched backward, spinning her longest arm beneath me. I sailed into the basket of leaves, the thin branches absorbing the force of my body, wrapping and cradling me, our limbs tangled together, the blood from my leg making pockmarks in the dusty soil below.

"I got eleven stitches. The doctor said it's going to scar. That means it's always going to be there."

"Well, if you would have listened to me..."

"I know...and thanks for catching me."

"Yeah, well...it's okay. It's always going to be there?"

"Yeah, always."

The maple waltzed with the soft summer wind, each tender rustle a reflection of elegance. For all of the times I had hidden beneath her shady umbrella, I had never noticed her beauty.

"Can you get a knife?" she asked.

"What do you want a knife for?"

"I just want one. It has to be sharp, though. Do you think you can get one?"

"Well, I guess. Yeah." I thought of my father's hunting knife that he kept in the back bottom drawer of his desk.

"Go get it."

"But what for?"

"Just go."

I returned with my father's folding knife and clicked out its stainless steel blade, avoiding its honed edge.

"Now what?"

"I want you to carve your name into me."

"What for?"

"Because as long as you do it right, it will be there forever. Just like your scar."

"But won't it hurt?"

"Probably. It has to."

"Then I won't do it. I'm not going to hurt you."

"It will only hurt for a while. Besides, then you will be a part of me, and that's all that I want. I love you."

I did not say anything. I ached to tell the maple that I wanted to be a part of her and that I would show everyone my whittled legacy. I wanted to tell her that I loved her, but, choking on my thoughts, I raised the knife to the height of my chest and dug the blade into the front of the maple.

The thick bark resisted even the smallest cuts of the knife. I pushed harder, but the sides of the blade were squeezed to a stop.

"You should clear away some of the bark first," she said.

I withdrew the knife, and using its pointed edge, I picked and scraped away pieces of the rough covering. Bit by bit, I stripped her surface with the focus of an archaeologist, peeling away the bark until I exposed a large patch of bare moist skin. Into this skin I sank the sharp blade. The wood gave way freely, the glistening steel grooving a twisted path through the surface. Winding and digging,

I whisked out my name with the speed of a woodsman.

"It's not deep enough," said the maple. Her voice fatigued from the pain. "I want it to stay. Make the letters deeper."

"I can't, not if it hurts you so much."

"Just finish." It was a demand. Her pain forcing her to conserve words, imploring me to complete my task.

Retracing my name, I scooped a deep ravine through each letter, brushing away the soft pulp with my hand, and the trenching yet deeper.

"Stop. Stop now." She was in agony.

I pulled away the knife and covered the cutting with my palm. She was silent as I looked up at her. I leaned forward and, removing my hand, I closed my eyes and pressed my lips against the moist skin. Then, resting my back against the maple, I sat on the ground.

"What does it feel like?" I asked.

"I don't know; it just hurts."

"I know, but what does it feel like?"

"I guess it feels like getting a tattoo."

"Oh... What does that feel like?"

"I don't know, it just hurts, that's all."

"Then why did you make me do it?"

"It's proof."

"Proof of what?"

"Of us. It's proof that we were together once, that we were here, and that we were good. I don't know what's going to happen. You don't know. I want to stay with you so badly, but what if we can't?"

I had never thought of this. Nothing I had ever known was final. School years or the seasons always blended in smooth spirals, each one leading to the next, always returning to the place where they started.

"But I love you."

"And I love you, too. So this way, no matter what, we will always be connected. I swear, even if we're apart, in fifty years I'll still think of you. I know it. And I'll have proof."

I laid back in the grass and I smiled as I began to understand what she meant. Stretching my arms flat over my head, I again looked up into the maple. Her lowest branches floated over me, one soft gesture of love and protection. I closed my eyes to the warm breezes of August and the gentle rustle of my sweet angel's wings.

Profound Reflection
by Marty Kraft

It was a winter morning in the early 1970's in Kansas City. I was returning from placing an ad in a neighborhood newspaper, offering my services as an ecological lifestyle counselor. I had struggled with the decision to be so bold as to think that I might help anyone change their life and I had finally gotten up the courage.

I was walking home feeling good for overcoming my fear, enjoying the bright sun and crisp air. I looked up to see a blue spruce in someone's yard and was moved by its beauty. I wandered around in my head for words and a phrase from *Psalms* came to mind and I said, "Lord, I love the beauty of Thy house and the place where Thy glory dwells."

At that instant, it was as if a mirror had been held up before my praising words. All over me bounced an incredible joy. Tears and laughter came spontaneously right there in the middle of the street. My chest swelled with warmth and felt like it was going to explode.

I looked around to see if anyone saw what I thought might appear as temporary insanity. I was alone. I walked on having learned something my mind could not understand.

Tree-Breath

by Forest Shomer

Thanksgiving, 1971, hours before the big community holiday meal at midmorning, I decided to climb from the Okanogan River Valley (north-central Washington State) to the ridge. Ascending many hundreds of vertical feet I walked into the frigid stillness. Nothing moved. As I left the valley the few sounds of living faded in the distance. Half-an-hour later I reached the top of the ridge and stopped, rested, and took in the vista of browned grass hillsides dotted with patches of snow. As I sat in the profound wintry silence, I became aware of a subtle sound. The sound of slow breathing. Cautiously, thinking about bear and cougar, I rose and surveyed the open range around me. There were no other animals present. The only life form of any size within 100 yards was...a large ponderosa pine tree.

Many years later, it still seems there was no possibility other than that I was hearing the sound of tree-breath.

Grandfather Cottonwoods
by Jackie Lee Hofer

I happen to live a few miles from the tallest (105 feet) and likely the largest (432 inches around the base) Plains cottonwood tree in the world. The tree is on private land and not open to the public. I did get permission about ten years ago to visit the tree. From the dirt roadway I could only see the upper branches, as it sits well below an earthen berm. Not until I crossed the berm and dry irrigation ditch did I get my first marvelous full view of this magnificent tree. The trunk was more than eleven feet across. I climbed onto its main junction where enormous branches splayed out in all directions. It was like being comforted by the granddaddy of all cottonwoods.

The male native cottonwood lives for about 100 years. Their thick trunks, rugged bark and huge limbs reach outward and upward in strengthening ways. The windy sound of their bright, shiny leaves is comforting, much like the sound of gentle waves on an ocean beach. These wise old trees speak of their staying power through the trying times of life. They withstand fierce winds and don't open their new leaves until the last freeze of winter has passed. Sometimes, the newer, less hardy, hybrid cottonless trees try to jump-start Spring by unfolding their leaves early, only to be chastised by a damaging frost.

I first experienced a cottonwood tree while living with my grandparents on a sharecropper farm near the Kansas/Oklahoma border. There were no other children to play with until Saturday afternoons when we drove seven miles to Kiowa, Kansas, to exchange milk and eggs for flour and sugar at the local grocery store. To entertain myself during the week, I listened to *The Lone Ranger* and *Superman* on the radio. Then with my faithful companion, Micky, a long-haired, white, mixed-breed dog, I headed for the gully and climbed onto the only tree on the farm—Grandfather Cottonwood. My imagination soared as my grandparents were too poor to own a television set to distract or lull me. This special tree was *my* tree—a lone boy and a lone, beckoning tree. I felt more alive and comforted in its embrace than any other place on the farm. I was an invincible superhero within its branches. Nothing could defeat me!

On a recent trip, I stayed in a primitive campground at Fort Robinson, Nebraska. I pitched the tent beneath the huge branch of an old growth cottonwood tree. I noticed later that several large branches had broken off sometime in its past—ones that could flatten a car, much less a ripstop nylon tent.

During the evening, a violent rain and windstorm blew in from the southwest with gusts above 75 miles per hour. I didn't want to move the tent even if I could have in that wind. So, I walked over to the cottonwood tree, placed my body and arms against its trunk and said, "Grandfather Cottonwood, I know you have been through many storms in life worse than this one, and I ask for your protection tonight." I awoke the next morning, the air was still, the rich, blue sky was without clouds, and the earth was refreshed and blessed. I was greeted with birdsong coming from the branches of the cottonwood tree. I thanked the tree for its strength and protection.

These Grandfather Cottonwood trees will pass on as do all grandfathers. But my cottonwood experiences will always be sweet ambrosia for my spirit.

Peace Trees
by *Walter Enloe*

Forty years ago I moved to Japan at the age of twelve. My parents were to work there as a minister and teacher for the next thirty years. I vividly remember visiting Peace Park and the Children's Monument a week after we moved to Hiroshima. Between the Children's Peace Monument and the Buddhist repository mound, where thousands of unidentified remains are buried, stands a grove of red maples. All have been planted over the past forty-five years at the epicenter of the Nuclear Age. They grow tall and straight in a place where it was assumed nothing would grow for ten thousand years. Students at the International School have made Peace Park their solemn playground; they all know what the place signifies about the past and they all have dreams for the future. No More Hiroshimas! No More Nagasakis!

One of the teachers, Mrs. Nobori, had been a young girl on August 6, 1945, and lived about three kilometers from this sacred place. The radiated winds of the firestorm blew down many of the wooden homes in her neighborhood. But what she remembers more than anything is that the terrific force of the explosion ripped and tore all the leaves off the trees in her yard and in the park next door. Many people made their way out of the atomic fire to this park. Later, the oleander bloomed, and that next spring in the atomic wasteland of Hiroshima, the leaves returned on some trees, and the cycle of life, like the Sphinx itself, arose out of the radioactive ashes. A monument stands in the corner dedicated to more than a thousand people cremated on this playground.

One of the survivors of that day of infamy was two-year-old Sadako Sasaki, who died folding paper cranes as symbols of longevity and her hope for a peaceful future. When she passed away at age twelve, the students in her class started a fund-raising campaign that built the Children's Monument and started the children's peace movement. With their anthem, "This is Our Cry: This is Our Wish for Peace in the World," they made the paper cranes a worldwide symbol. Sadako's spirit lived on. Years later, the International School supported this movement by writing a book that told Sadako's story, and with the help of UNESCO spread her story around the world. Today, the monument is covered in tens of thousands of paper cranes with banners from classrooms from many countries.

When the International School's K-1 class arrived at Peace Park, there were 14 five- and six-year-olds from ten countries. They had brought their cranes. They placed them at the monument. Then Mai yelled out, "Are those the peace trees?"

Her teacher nodded.

"Can we?" Aisha asked, and they all ran into the grove and found a tree.

"I'm hugging mine." "Look, I can get my arms all the way around." "I'm going to kiss mine." "I like this one and this one, too." "Look, I'm a peace tree!" "Teacher, where is yours?"

The teacher pointed to one and then another and then she pointed to all the children.

The teacher gathered them together next to the monument dedicated to the thousands of students who were killed. They sat under a tree that was festooned with garlands of paper cranes and with bits of folded paper prayers wrapped around the tree's twigs all at different points of decay. Their teacher told them, "You are my peace trees. God made the trees and plants and then people gathered leaves from them to make paper. Look up here into the tree's branches. On some of that paper, priests write prayers and they are folded and put into trees like those up there. Over seven years the papers disintegrate and turn into dust from which other plants and trees will grow. And so life goes round and round like a spiral—nature, people, nature."

"Are these peace trees children trees?" a child asked.

"Children and adults," their teacher suggested.

"Some are parents," Serene said.

"All are teachers!" Isaac noted.

The great cycle of life arises out of our continued human destruction and madness. But there is hope in this Post-modern lifetime. If each child finds and loves her peace tree like herself and her friends, she makes a difference. And then there is the hope of the children—that adults will find their peace trees, too. Feel the breeze of Sadako's peaceful spirit alive and well within and among the peace trees.

I wish I had learned to hug trees forty years ago; perhaps peacemaking and stewardship would have become a part of my life much earlier. I now know that what I first experienced in Hiroshima forty years ago has affected everything I have felt and imagined since then. For with its misery and pain there has been insight and illumination. I know, too, that I had to wait many years for these children to teach me.

Chapter Three

Trees of Childhood

I think that I shall never see,
A poem lovely as a tree.
A tree whose hungry mouth is prest
Against the earth's sweet flowing breast;
A tree that looks at God all day
And lifts her leafy arms to pray;
A tree that may in Summer wear
A nest of robins in her hair;
Upon whose bosom snow has lain;
Who intimately live with rain.
Poems are made by fools like me,
But only God can make a tree.
—*Joyce Kilmer*

A Tree Remembered
by J. P. Dancing Bear

This tree speaks a language
none can deny
I look out through branches
listening to her song
She is a mother of rings
a witness to the earth changes
the old rivers and lakes
that once moved here
Of men and machines
that tore away the hills
and made this place suburbia
Lucky some say
she stands before this house
like a sentinel
watching me grow
watching my changes
My five summers' friend
I have been climbing all over her
studying her every contour
naming and feeding
the squirrels and birds
that live with her
careful not to break a single branch
Eleven years old
to her hundreds
never a greater team will ever be
than me and this tree.

Mimosas

by Laura C. Martin

Though many people seemed to have learned all they needed to know of life in kindergarten, I learned my most important lessons perched high above my childhood home, safe within the embracing arms of a mimosa tree. There were two mimosas, actually, one in the front and another in the back. They towered high above the roof of the house, their outstretched limbs almost, but not quite, touching. As a young child, I thought the two trees were married. As I changed from a trusting child to an imaginative teen, and read one romance novel after another, I dreamed that they had been separated as seedlings and had spent a lifetime searching for one another. Finally, they soared above the roofline and the tips of their branches brushed against one another, like lovers whose fingertips touch and whose souls are joined.

Though both were good climbing trees, it was the front yard tree that neared perfection. The bottom branches were thick, sturdy and low enough, so that even my short child's legs could swing over. I could pull myself up for the first step of a daily journey into the world of twigs and branches and leaves that never failed to yield a singular joy.

The leaves were like thick eyelashes, deeply divided and attached to a center vein with a stem the width of a hair. Each spring the trees would bloom a bubble bath foam of pink flowers. They were soft as a cloud and touched with a fragrance sweeter than that of a rose. During the weeks of bloom, I wore these pink powder puff blossoms tucked behind my ear, strung together as a necklace or carefully woven into the hem of my shirt. They transformed me from a skinny-legged child with scabby knees to a regal princess of incomparable grace and beauty.

As my legs grew longer and stronger, my spirit and courage also grew. I climbed higher and higher into the limbs until I could see for miles around. I was queen over all I could see. My view extended past the roofs of my friend's houses, past the schoolyard, and past the steeple of our church. From my tree perch, I could see into distant lands, as both past and future came within my line of sight. From the treetop, I was able to try on a hundred different lives, and on any given day I was a doctor, a teacher, a missionary, a poet, an artist. From the safety of my tree, I could sing opera, preach sermons, win marathons. With bark beneath my bare legs and hands clutching the smooth, rounded limbs, I was home-coming queen, valedictorian and gymnastics champion.

Not all was fantasy in my tree haven, though, for I learned very real lessons as well. I learned that life is precarious when you go far out on a limb. I learned that it takes courage to climb high and is exhilarating when you neared the top. I also learned that what goes up, be it a factor of fear, hunger or gathering darkness, must come down. I found that being down was not all bad, though, for it allowed me to dream of climbing again another day.

I have to admit, I was not always faithful to my mimosa. I played the field but I quickly learned that although other trees might be more exotic and more beautiful, my mimosa, with its deep roots and strong foundation, was safe and dependable. Through the years, I learned to appreciate its beauty in all seasons. Although I loved springtime blooms, I also learned to love the bare winter branches.

Like a panacea, the tree gave me whatever I needed. From this tree I harvested consolation and companionship, as well as the excitement of a challenge and the thrill of climbing past comfort. It was here that the leaves dried my tears and the tree allowed me to forget my childhood troubles as branch after branch stair-stepped toward the sky, challenging me to test nerve, strength and flexibility. Each year I climbed higher, yet I never did climb all the way to the top. I always thought I would, but something, whether it was the practicality of a trunk narrowing to flimsy limbs or the desire to be in the tree rather than above it, kept me within the safety and obscurity of the lower, thick branches heavy with leaves and blossoms.

I thought my tree would always be there—a bastion of strength, a living reminder of the joyful days of childhood. But as my teen years dissolved into adulthood, a blight ravaged mimosas throughout the neighborhood. First the backyard tree, then the one in front succumbed, slowly weakened and died. I cried of course; who would not at such a loss? But like the dozens of teachers who touched my life, then disappeared never to be seen again, my tree remains in my memory as beautiful and magical as it was the day my father first swung me up into the leafy branches and allowed me to sit there all by myself.

The lessons of the mimosa have been life lessons for me. Through the tree, first in reality and then in memory, I became aware of my connection to the earth and of my kinship with all living things. It was while sitting in this tree with the world at my feet that I first began to accept the challenge of putting down roots while still soaring toward heaven.

Branches of Delight
by Robert C. Fuentes

As a child, the street I lived on sat smack in between the freeway on one end and the railroad tracks on the other. With five older brothers and sisters to add to the situation, it did not take me long to learn that moments of peace in my life would be precious and few.

Hence, it was my surprise to discover that climbing the elm tree in our backyard during summer could take me to another world.

There, nestled within its limbs, I would float off to sleep, away from the train whistles and car horns, barking dogs and screaming children. The cool breezes fanned away the day's heat as the leaves sang the soothing tune of nature to my soul.

That tree remained my best kept secret and friend. When it spoke in silent whispers, I listened, learning more about myself than I could have otherwise.

My parents sold their house on my twenty-third birthday. By my twenty-fourth, the new owners had cut down the tree and sold it for firewood. But, to this day, I know that its roots are buried there deep in the ground alongside mine.

Elm Tree Moment
by Robert C. Fuentes

Today they fell the elm tree of my youth;
The place I more than once
grabbed hold of its thick branch of hope
so that I might swing above the ground,
feet dangling above the world
of bottle caps and bubble gum
I knew so well…
My head so much closer to heaven
that even the air smelled sweeter.
There I held on
with all of my strength
long after all blood left my arms,
leaving my small white knuckles
to betray my grip by letting go
one finger at a time,
until finally
I could hold on no longer
no matter how hard I tried;
and would fall like a leaf to earth
with only thoughts of happiness
and memories such as these
to last me a lifetime
throughout the seasons
of my life's changes.

Tree Companions
by Teresa W. Wolfe

Trees speak to me. They always have, at some level, but I've only recently become aware of it.

For many years, I resolutely refused to listen.

When I was a child, my family lived in a house across the street from a large estate which had been built earlier in the century by some of the richest forefathers of our city. The estate had three buildings: a castle (literally!), a livery stable and a servant's quarters. The buildings and the wall surrounding the estate were made of quarried limestone. At the time I lived across the street, the owners of the estate had already passed on. The property had been donated to the Omaha Department of Public Education and converted into office space and conference rooms.

The estate was about two city blocks square in size. There were many trees on the property. My brother, Bill, and I spent most of our free time in those trees, with specific games and fantasies attached to our favorites.

There was the "Bonus" tree, with a lone board nailed high in the branches, where we used to watch the sun rise and set. We also had a game that we played with this tree. We would dig old nylon stockings (pre-panty hose days) out of garbage cans, fill the toes with gravel and small rocks, tie off the toes and swing the stockings round and round, letting them fly into the tree to get caught on the branches. The goal was to get them caught on the highest, outermost branches. After we had caught several, we'd then have to climb the tree and retrieve them. This was no small feat, as the branches were 20-30 feet up, with a cement street below.

The "Family" tree (my favorite) had large resting spots among the branches. I would go there to do my homework after school or just when I wanted to be alone. I would often sit up there and sing. The tree was located in the parking lot, toward the entrance. My after school moments there coincided with the employees leaving work. Sometimes I would look down while I was singing in the branches to see people standing there watching me. It never occurred to me to wonder what they must be thinking. (Only in childhood are we so secure within ourselves.)

The tree where we played house (surprisingly not the "Family" tree) had several long, horizontally running branches that turned abruptly vertical at the end. My friends, brother, and I each had our own branch, with our "rooms" at the end.

Then there was the Ginkgo tree. We loved the sound of the name! We would chant Ginkgo over and over. I loved its smooth bark and its fan shaped leaves. It was an old tree with several thick, high-reaching branches. We had a great view of the city from its topmost branches. Unfortunately, it was located right outside the main door and we were often spotted by the "powers that be" who would invariably scold us and make us get down.

The Mulberry tree was a squat, multibranched tree that we generally only climbed when the berries were ripe. Mom could always tell when we had been playing in the Mulberry tree because our lips and the bottoms of our feet would all be stained. (Any veteran tree climber can attest that the best way to climb trees is barefoot.)

The property also had a Magnolia tree. It was actually more of a shrub than a tree and not a particularly good climbing tree, but I loved the rich, sweet, heady smell of the blossoms.

In retrospect, I realize that trees played a large part in my childhood. It was only when I was asked to write this story (thank you, Karen) that I recognized that they are important figures in my life. I love their energy, strength, flexibility and silent endurance as the daily chaos of life races by. Finally, I am ready and eager to listen. I can see much wisdom in trees.

Did my childhood frolicking in all those trees influence my later decision to become an herbalist? I never stopped to contemplate it before, and it doesn't matter now. That awareness pales in comparison to their truer impact on my life.

Trees did, and do, influence my spiritual unfolding, however. They are quiet, knowing companions in my quest to discover my spiritual self. They offered me their special energies throughout my childhood. They stood quietly, lovingly during my years of denial and discovery. They reach out to me constantly, now that I am ready to hear their song. For this I am eternally grateful.

Things I Believed When I Was Eight
by Claudia Van Gerven

I believed the trees were alive like people. When you put your hand on the limbs of old apple trees, they feel like flesh—warm, sentient mother's flesh. I believed everyone believed this. Or maybe that's just what I believe now, middle-aged without an apple tree. I remember myself as a girl in a dress, my bare feet dangling down, sitting in the ample lap of an old apple tree in my grandfather's orchard. The sun was warm on apple flesh, on girl flesh. I believe I was happy or at least I like to believe I was happy. I believe that when I put my hand on those smooth limbs, grey-brown like morning doves, someone held me in her arms, someone whispered low, someone hummed, someone radiant and awesome murmured, "yes, yes."

In Which She Discovers She Has Always Been a Witch

by Claudia Van Gerven

—for Tara

I have always talked to trees
and their answers have unfurled
under my skin like leaves.
Wind has nested in my hair
ever since I can remember.
Birds dive into my sleep
to fish for silvery bits of dream.
I have tasted air
with my tongue.

When I was eight I lived
a whole summer in the arms
of an ancient apple tree.
I have put my small grimy hands
on savory brown flesh,
felt the warm, regular thumping
of her heartbeat.
I lost my shoes and my fear
of the mossy folds in the crutch.
I could climb as high
as my breath rose.
I was so happy
in my own face
God could never
evict me.

Wood Carving Teacher

by Clara Courteau

I am afraid of heights; so climbing was never something I did unless I had to, but climbing my pear tree was an exception. This tree was in front of my childhood home in Missouri. This tree was a centerpiece in our lives. It shaded the house from the hot afternoon sun and was a haven when you were too warm from working in the large gardens. Underneath the pear tree was where we would sit on a summer Sunday afternoon when we had company. But, most of all, it was an irresistible place to play whenever we had the chance. Its limbs were spaced so that even a small child could climb if an older brother could be coaxed into helping you reach that first branch. You could climb and climb until you reached the sky (at least eight or ten feet) or it seemed that way when climbing is so hard to do.

After I grew up and left home, the pear tree died and was replaced by a maple tree. It was forgotten until many years later when I was home on vacation. While I was out walking, I found an old weathered stump lying in a fencerow almost hidden by weeds. It was the remainder of my pear tree. In the years between, I had learned to appreciate wood as one of the most beautiful and useful of materials. I had become a wood-carver and wood-turner, and I was always looking for different woods to use in my projects. Here was a perfect example of what I wanted to find, a piece of wood with beauty and memories. I brought it back to my home in Minnesota and cut it into pieces. From two of the pieces I turned rustic bowls. These bowls are a centerpiece of my displays at woodcarving shows. I have so much fun telling about the days I climbed that tree as a little girl.

Little White Stones
by Carol Fjeld

Behind our house there were woods
Just past the bright waving white sheets
And the bike rack made of skinny trees
Where the ground was always moist
It was dark and cool, black browns
And deep greens, damp dirt
And rotting bark, earthy sweet
Trees softly breathing
Inviting us into quiet play
Leaving the banging screen doors
And little girl differings behind
Soft drops of sun rained in
We didn't have to squint to see
Our eyes could widen there
In this place where we made believe
A village, we called it,
Houses made of sticks and sprigs
Our yards grew fat moss
Lined with little white stones
With great care we built and groomed
Little hands smoothing roads between
The houses where no people ever lived.
We didn't seem to mind that
No one was ever home. We knew
They would have complicated things.

The Climbing Tree
by Richard Risemberg

I grew from child to man in a white clapboard house in Hollywood. The street was quiet and little-traveled by cars back then, lined by flat green lawns and mute houses almost identical to ours. If you looked north from our front porch you could see the low brown hills that hold up the famous Hollywood sign. A little to the right of that were the three green domes of the Griffith Observatory. The width of the street and the paucity of human forms, so typical of a city where people drive instead of walk, made the quietness of Lucerne Boulevard expressive of dullness rather than tranquility. When the summer hazes filled the sky and all the shadows vanished, time seemed to disappear. The day endured changeless and featureless, until at a moment that seemed controlled more by clock than nature, the light faded away overhead and the streetlights came on. There were few other children in the neighborhood and it was pointless to stay out front.

The backyard was equally unremarkable, the usual rectangle of listless grass bordered with half-desiccated flowers and some tall, severely trimmed shrubs, which separated us from the backyards next door. There was, however, a gnarled olive tree in almost the exact center of the yard. Its roots humped up like buttresses. The knobby trunk provided handholds for even a clumsy climber like myself. Eight or ten feet above the ground, the trunk divided into four thick branches that reached outward and upward in sturdy disorder, in the way of olives. There were several comfortable sitting places at different levels, and three or four children could stay up in the tree for quite a long time without crowding each other. The leaves were not so thick that you felt shrouded from the world. You could see the roofs and yards that were hidden to you when you were on the ground, but the California sun did not bear on you uncomfortably. If no one else were around to play with, it was still a good place to be. Leaning on a rough branch ten feet above the ground, you could be out of sight but not isolated. One or another of my cats would often join me up there, stretched out with eyes half-closed on the horizontal branch that pointed toward the kitchen window. Our family was a turbulent one, but there was always peace in the tree.

Many years later my mother, then living alone in the house, cut down the tree so she could put in a swimming pool. She has never learned how to swim, but feels that a pool is more "classy" than a tree. My son has often played in that pool, splashing noisily and diving for coins that his grandmother throws into the water for him, but he has never had a climbing tree for himself. The closest he has come was one summer when he spent several hours each day up on the garage roof, alone with a book or sometimes with a friend. We have planted trees in our own backyard, not far from his grandmother's house, but he will be grown before the trees are tall.

Hidden Up
by C. B. Follett

In the center of the yard,
like a gift from Jack and his six beans,
is a chestnut worthy of the village smithy.

Its trunk is vast and it crowns
well above the third story and the roof.
Each spring it unfurls mittens of downy celadon

that turn into green spaniel ears,
and white spikes of flowers
shoot up like fountains.

Once I learn to get up that tree;
once I creep and climb
behind the shadow of leaves,

even my movements are hidden.
From the kitchen window I hear
family voices murmur; from the porch

the creak of wicker,
squeak of the green glider
as legs swing them in adult rhythms.

In my tree I am sailing the South Pacific,
fighting enemies in jungles and small villages,
capturing spies and bandits

as the sun takes its slow and ponderous course
dappling through branches until it reaches
the break in the leaves that means supper.

Of Mulberry Trees and Lightning Strikes
by Cynthia A. Arnett

Mine was a Mulberry tree in western Kentucky, on a little farm in Cairo, just outside Henderson.

That Mulberry tree was huge when I was a little girl. My earliest memories are those of a big old branch coming off one side that held wood-slat chain-link swings for my little sister, Carol, and myself. The ground just beneath the swings was worn bare and slick. The shade provided by the thickly-leaved branches kept the ground cool as could be even on a hot July afternoon.

One year, and I really do not remember exactly when, a bolt of lightning hit that Mulberry tree and split it in two. If my Daddy was concerned it was going to split further and land on the house, he sure didn't show it. So the Mulberry tree continued to live on even growing branches off the two split parts.

As my sister and I grew older, another sister and three brothers came into the picture. In our efforts to provide ourselves with something fun to do besides dirt-clod dodgeball in the cornfields, we collected discount coupons from the local Ben Franklin store for the traveling carnival held in their parking lot. We did ride the real rides in town, but our pockets were full of the strips of red and blue paper "tickets" when we got home.

Right down the middle of the split in one stumped branch, we nailed a couple of nails purposefully bent to be used as "controls." One of us would be the person "in charge of the rides," name two or three different rides available, and collect the tickets. Then another one of us would stand behind the swings, working with the "one in charge" and either spin furiously, jerk haphazardly, or swing to the sky the kids who would have a ticket for their ride of choice. Those were some of the best carnival experiences I have ever had.

There was a time when poison ivy grew up one side of the Mulberry tree. My grandmother dumped salt on it so we would not have to spend the summer covered pink with calamine lotion. That tree must have taken care of me because I never got poison ivy when playing in its branches and between the two split trunks.

Years later, another bolt of lightning hit that Mulberry tree and split one of the trunks into another two. Now that Mulberry tree had three trunks. Still my Daddy did not try to take it down even though it was awfully close to the house.

Today, some 40-plus years later, when I go back to Cairo to visit my folks' home, that Mulberry tree is still there. The three trunks and their branches are still green in the spring and strong in the winter. The ground beneath where the two swings were is just as cool as can be even on a hot July afternoon.

Backyard Tree
by Lisa Fay

When I was young and at play,
I hung on a tree
wide as a petticoat
high above the worries
dreams away from the ropes of authority
in woods as open as Fenway
and tried to pop
a balloon sky.

Not yet nine,
my friends and I
signed off to college
before writing our first papers,
hitting our first home runs
or reveling in the first wet kisses.
Our parents deemed us adults
before our first periods.

In the only tree gramps planted,
I took care not to break the branches,
his arms ferociously hugging me.
It wasn't as though I was unloved,
just that I needed so much love.
Sitting among those branches
a new leaf stuck in my hair;
home is not responsible
for all the love needed.

The Lesson of the Kapok Tree
by Susana Bouquet-Chester

"It's not a kapok," I protested. "My friends here call it a 'caroleeena' tree, with a long eee, like in Spanish."

"It's a kapok," my father insisted. "Later in the year it gets fuzzy all over. Only kapoks do that. Those children don't know what they're talking about."

So we called it The Kapok. Its majestic outline stood against the distant view of Havana, Cuba. The intense ultramarine sea colored its backdrop.

I loved that tree more than anything else. Back in my childhood, it was my best friend. Often, I disappeared from the house to climb The Kapok. I grabbed its lowest branch, swung my legs around it and pulled myself up to a sitting position. But that place was never high enough for me. Like a little monkey, I scrambled up to my favorite spot where a branch crossed two others, making a "v" small enough for me to sit on without falling through. I was so used to climbing that I could have done it with my eyes closed.

This was a special place, high enough to receive the full breezes from the ocean. It was a secret place, where I could sing lullabies without being heard. Sitting there, my hands and my soul were free. I was truly in paradise.

My mother stood on the house veranda drying her hands, and, as usual, cautioned me in French, her native tongue.

"Fais bien attention!" "Be very careful!"

And, as usual, I gave the same answer, "Oui, Maman."

She went back inside and set me free to stay with my friend.

In the secrecy of my hideaway, I hugged the tree, but my arms reached only half around. I caressed its smooth, grayish bark, admired the solid body and the beautiful jutting of the branches into the air. "I want to be just like you," I said softly. "Strong and beautiful."

I leaned my head against the trunk and listened, as I always did. That day I thought the tree answered me. I thought I could feel its sap race upward, coursing with a heartbeat. It's alive. Just like me. Then somehow I made the connection: if I grew, and reached for the stars, I could become strong and beautiful. What a revelation! I was just a little girl, but I knew I'd found an answer. I marveled at the wisdom of the tree and determined that I would be just like it— strong and beautiful.

How long did I stay there? I don't remember exactly. Probably all afternoon. It takes at least that long to assimilate the great aha's of one's life. Mother would have thought that I was wasting the day, but after all, back then, I did have all the time in the world.

Now, fifty years later, I visit Cuba and I go to our old homestead. The hurricane of '35 swept the house away. I greet my old friend. It seems smaller now. Parts of it are broken, but it still stands, without leaves or flowers, against the same magnificent view of Havana.

Is this the tree that held me in its arms, its branches my cradle? Is this the tree that heard my songs?

The breezes blow and the leaves in the brambles murmur a sort of melody—do I hear my long forgotten lullaby?

A Tree

by Peg Lopata

They say it's unusual to remember anything of your childhood before the age of four. At about four, language starts to define your world. Before that, you have only your senses. So if you remember anything before then, it's embedded in the memory of your body.

I know I was not yet four when I first fell in love. I know my first love was a tree, although at the time I might have thought it was three trees. She cradled me in the cup between her three trunks. Her three arms were always open, firmly attached to the wide barrel of her footing. She stood vigilant and faithful, anchored in the back corner of the rectangle of grass behind our house in the Bronx. I used her in times of terror to hide from cruel brothers, angry mothers and the many other thorns of life. She was my guardian.

The Bronx was an unlikely place to fall in love with a tree. It was a place more known for its abandoned tenements, garbage-covered vacant lots and graffiti-covered trains. But Morgan Avenue, the place I spent the first seven years of my life, was far from the mean streets. I felt lucky to be there because of that towering pillar with the fluffy green head that grew in the corner of our backyard.

Our house was a stone's throw from the edge of a parkway that was truly a "park" way. The green space was wider than the road space. In front of each house was a tree and a narrow or square garden. The road wasn't paved suburban smooth; so there were plenty of stones to play with. I had no idea my birthplace was a city.

My earliest memory of this tree, my love, is sensual and textural. I can remember the scratchy bark picking at my shoulder blades and my pale baby-skin knees resting gently in front of me, each leaning against a section of the tree. It had once been one tree, one trunk and then it had divided into three. It must have been a young tree when it had suffered this split, because each trunk was now large, solid and equal in size. It was a perfect trinity to hold me.

Above me was a mass of spring-green leaves, frolicking back and forth, continually letting blue flakes of sky mingle and merge with lemony verdant green and eye-squinting shots of gold. When I tipped my head back it fell between the space of two trunks and I was swinging without the swing, dangling in a swirling, visible atmosphere. Here was my heaven, in this tree's great chasm, held by a giant with three knees who said, "Look up, look up."

I shared my body and soul with this tree in a love so interior, so nameless and so boundless that she told me the secrets of the universe, so that I could laugh out loud in her sanctuary, down close to the roots of her beginnings and the meaning of existence. I met God here and I can thank my tree for the introduction and induction. She captured my soul and handed it to God to keep.

The soul of a child is a flighty thing. Each night it escapes the confines of the body, winging off to a star to tell a story or hear a song. Before the soul lands permanently and gladly, it does not belong to us or the child. It travels almost as easily as a speck of dust. My soul landed most gently and with the greatest welcome in a tree. That tree is my first memory. A tree that held more than my body. A tree that gave me reason to be here and endurance to stay.

Postscript: The tree on Morgan Avenue that I loved is still there, some forty years past. She has lost one section, but is enormous and still thriving.

Chapter Four

Children's Tree Stories

I am the Lorax,
I speak for the trees,
for the trees have no tongues.
—*Dr. Seuss*

Tree House

by Casey Gilmartin

Kabooomm! The Sweetgum tree in my backyard split and crashed down in the windy rain storm. After the storm was over, my dad climbed a ladder fifteen feet up the tree trunk to where it split. He was surprised to find that the trunk, which was three feet in diameter, was hollow all the way to the ground with about a four inch thick wall. He had a great idea.

Dad was cutting the top part of the tree off when I walked outside one Saturday morning. He planned to build a tree house on the trunk. I was excited. My whole family worked on building the tree house for several weeks. When we finally finished, it was the coolest tree house I had ever seen.

My dad cut an arched door, two feet wide and four feet tall, in the tree trunk. The door was hinged and had a chain handle. To get up to the tree house, we climbed a metal fire escape ladder up the inside of the trunk and pushed open the trap door in the floor of the tree house. Our new house was five feet tall and eight feet long by five feet wide. Two sides of the house were open with a railing and a third side had a small window. One of the open sides looked out over the creek in our backyard.

My best friend, Gina, who lived across the creek from me, loved to come over and play in my tree house. We had lunch up there a lot during the summers. We created a "pulley" which was a bucket attached to a rope. That's how we got our food up to the tree house. Gina and I had great fun up there except for one time when I was climbing up the slippery metal ladder. On the very last rung at the top, my foot slipped and I fell thirteen feet to the ground. I sprained my ankle and ended up on crutches for two weeks.

I was sad to leave my tree house when my family had to move closer to Paideia. I wish we could've moved the tree and the tree house. I have pictures and memories, and I will never forget my tree house.

The Ohio Mushroom Tree
by Meghan McKeon

When I was seven years old, I lived in Shaker Heights, Ohio. It was a very nice part of Ohio, where the city council was involved in the cleanliness of the town. All the sidewalks were even. There were dog walking regulations, and signs weren't allowed in your yard. There were many trees and plants in Shaker Heights, yet none of them could compare with the one tree in my front yard. It was a small tree shaped like a little green mushroom. It was the perfect size and shape to play in. When the branches grew long, they were like a curtain that I could hide behind. The tree was small yet it stood so proud and beautiful between all the other tall trees that surrounded it. This was my tree.

When my friends came over we would play in the yard and in the tree. The tree was just tall enough for my friends and I to hang by our knees on the branches, suspended in the air. We would peel the seed pods that were on the ground and throw them in the air. The pods would come down spinning like a helicopter. My friends and I had contests to see how many pods would land on the mushroom tree. To do this, the wind had to be just right. The little, green mushroom tree was like a playmate to me.

Every day I would play in this tree. Flowers would come out all over it in the spring, and the sweet smell of perfume would dance in the air. The flowers would grow apart in some places and make windows in my little mushroom castle. I would put the flowers in my hair and look out my windows at the world outside. The long branches hid my feet from view and made me feel safe. When I was sad, I would sit at the base of the tree and tell it all my troubles. Sometimes when the leaves were falling, I would make a little carpet of leaves around the tree and sit on it, just enjoying the quiet. This was my tree.

The Cumberland Tree
by Kathryn "Kat" Rasche

Ever since I've gone to Cumberland Island, Georgia, there is a tree I've always loved. Every time I go to Cumberland Island I usually spend most of my time climbing it. When I go, I don't always just go with my family, but with a few others. One of the families has two boys, Matt and Will, and we all love to climb this tree. It has so many branches coming out of the trunk and they stretch out very far. There aren't a lot of trees that are close around it and sometimes its branches get stuck in other trees. Will, Matt and I each have a section of the tree that we own. We can't go on each other's sections unless they say you can. I have a really neat section because there is one branch that you can climb up, and if you climb up it far enough there is a little seat. I always go up there when I get on the tree. Matt also has a really cool section because his branches go up and there are little places that you can put your feet to climb up them and get to the top of the tree. Will also has a cool section because there is a low-lying limb on the tree, but it stretches over a little shower that is for people just to rinse off with when they come off of the beach. He is able to pull the string that is attached to it and then the water will come out. A few times he used it to threaten people, like he would say, "Don't get close to this tree because if you do I will spray you." It always seemed to make them go away because they thought he was weird or something.

Next to this tree is a little log that is standing upwards. One day someone came and chopped wood off of it on one side and now it is like a little seat. It faces toward the tree and you can sit on the wood seat and just look at the tree for hours. It has such wonderful texture and its limbs look like a family tree. They have a few branches at the top and each of those branches has a couple more branches on them, and so on.

This tree reminds me of my life, because the first time I went to Cumberland it wasn't as big as it is now, and every time I've gone back to Cumberland and seen this tree it has always grown a little bit if not a lot from what it had looked like before. And each time I go there I have grown more and more.

Its branches seem to be reaching out and trying to give you a great big hug. It feels like it just wants you to come and climb its branches and play in it.

A lot of trees that I have known have been cut down. But one thing I'm glad for is this tree has never been cut down. I love this tree very much and I hope it will never be cut down. It is a very wonderful tree.

My Tree Story
by Graham Bonner

There is a tree that is on a trail next to my house. This tree is a great big oak tree that is fifty-five feet high in the air with a swing on it. The first time I saw the tree, I was three years old. I got on the swing and swung for a long time. For one of my birthdays, my friends and I played Man Hunt and the tree would be the base. It is fun playing games around it.

When you look around the tree there is a creek by it. Across the creek there is a big patch of bamboo. My friends and I like to eat the leaves like the Pandas do.

My godfather sometimes walks his dog on the trail and I swing on the swing. The tree has real big roots. Sometimes I trip over the roots. It doesn't hurt that much. So I just get back up and start to play again. You can get very lost on the trail.

One time my friends and I were playing Man Hunt. My friend went off the trail and got in the creek and hid. We couldn't find him for an hour. Finally, he decided to come out of hiding. He couldn't find where he was. He went back up the creek the way he came calling out our names. When he knew where he was, he was standing under the big tree while we were off looking for him. When we came back he was swinging and grinning as wide as a mile. We asked him, "Where were you?" He said, "I was hiding in the creek and I got lost, so I followed the creek to the oak tree."

I have a lot of stories about the tree. I know some night I want to go camping under the swing. My favorite and most funny story was when my friend wanted to swing really far. So I pushed him really hard. He got real high in the air. He lost his grip and fell into the bamboo trees. He was not hurt, but he said, "I felt like George of the Jungle."

Sometimes I try to hug the tree but my arms are too small to cover it.

My Tree Experience
by Katherine Johnson

When I was in first grade, I used to go to my friend Eleanor's house where we would go to her neighbor's yard and scurry over to a tall magnolia tree. This tree had huge, green, smooth, slick leaves that were attached to big, wide, thick, sturdy branches that surrounded the tree. The tree towered above us as we pushed our way through the bunches of branches.

When we finished making our way through the branches, we looked up. It seemed like the tree was a huge umbrella. It was like we were in the rain forest under the big canopy. The vines of the tree seemed like wild jungle vines. We wouldn't be surprised if we even saw a huge leopard appear from behind the tree.

Its shadows surrounded us as we pounced up onto the first branch. Then we made our way up to where we usually sat, the low, middle of the tree. After we were comfortable, we would either chat, play with the neighbor's cat, who also was drawn to the tree, or we would do a movie series called "Masters of the Tree."

Now that I come to think of it, "Masters of the Tree" was really dumb! You see, my friend and I pretended we had our own movie company. "Masters of the Tree" was the first movie that started our company. I would be this female explorer that found this tree in the rain forest. My friend would pretend to be a boy who lived in the tree. Things went on normally until I found out about the villain. The villain was really invisible, but in our imaginations, he looked kind of like Darth Vader. If you climbed on top of the tree roots, the villain would come after you. That's just a sampling of the so called "movie." The rest is way too stupid to tell.

One time, I even fell off the great tree. It felt sort of like a kiddy roller coaster, but all I could see was a huge blur of tree branches. When I was falling off the tree, it took me awhile to realize the fact that I was really falling. I didn't really know what had hit me. One minute I was sitting on a not-so-sturdy branch talking, the next minute I was falling. I hit the the ground on my back. I was lucky the ground was dirt, not cement. For about two seconds I couldn't breathe, but then I was back to my old self again. I even said out loud, "That was fun!" No injuries or anything, except for the gash on my knee, which wasn't really that notice-able. The next time I came over we still played on the tree but I was careful.

We also used the tree as a hiding spot to hide from my friend's mom and her sister. We could see the trespassers through the gaps between the branches, but they couldn't see us. Eventually, we would begrudgingly get off the tree.

We could have stayed up on the big tree for hours and hours. We could have stayed up there for days and days. We really, I mean really, loved that tree. By the time when we hit late second or early third grade, the idea of sitting around on a tree got sort of lame. Eventually people grow out of things; we grew out of the tree.

The tree is still here today, except we don't really climb it that much. We talk about it a lot, though. We also talk about the stupid "Masters of the Tree" movie. Still, it was fun when we were in first grade. Sometimes we do climb the tree, very rarely though. Now we're off to different fads.

Tree Story
by Shruti Parekh

One of my favorite trees, a dogwood, stands proudly at the edge of my front yard. The tree, with a cinnamon brown trunk, has light green leaves dangling from the branches. Medium-sized with tons of low branches, it happens to be great for climbing and swinging. There is a small step, a part of the tree that juts out, where I can place my foot and easily climb up to the branches. I love to climb up and rest there.

When spring comes, my tree grows little white flowers which look like snowflakes. In the fall, the leaves turn to a reddish color, followed by bare branches when the leaves fall off. Once I thought of making a swing on one of the branches, but that was a long time ago. All that is hanging there since then is a piece of string. I also wanted to make a tree house, but I wasn't sure if one would fit with all those branches extending out everywhere. Anyway, I like it the way it is.

There is one spot in the tree where I love to hang out. It's a big branch that goes straight up. In the middle, another branch reaches out horizontally forming a comfortable seat with a backrest. The tree forms a canopy of shade, which makes it a pleasant place to be. I really like my dogwood because I can do so many things in it— play little imaginary games with friends, climb, swing and just rest. It is like an old friend to me because I have played in it for such a long time.

One time, maybe three years ago, my friend and I were outside playing with those small animal toys that I think are called Pretty Pets. She had a cat and I had a bird. We pretended that the tree was their home and they would visit each other and play. We had a really great time. Without the tree, there would have been no home for the bird and the cat.

When I am by myself, I usually just sit on one of the tree branches and watch cars go by. This spot is so peaceful. On good days, a soft breeze blows the leaves around. It is pure bliss, sitting there in the shade, with a cool breeze blowing. The place is so comfortable and quiet that I can just sit there and think about everything and anything that I want without anyone disturbing me. And if I'm not comfortable, there are so many other branches to choose from to get comfortable. Even on hot summer days, it's my favorite spot since there is so much shade. Besides, not as many mosquitoes get me because they are usually around the grass, and being up in the tree, I'm away from the grass.

Just about all the people on my street are elderly; so they don't come out of their houses that often. But every now and then their children or grandchildren come for a visit and I can casually sit in my tree and watch them without being noticed.

When one of my friends comes, we usually climb the tree together and watch people and cars or simply talk. It is easy for anyone to climb quite high because there are so many sturdy branches. I really love my tree since it is such a wonderful place to play and rest. I've liked that tree ever since I moved into my house four years ago.

The Fire Tree
by Elizabeth S. Pembleton

I once loved a tree but it got ruined. This tree was a very tall tree; in fact, it was the tallest tree by my aunt and uncle and my three cousins' house. This tree was not the best looking tree; it was just a normal pine. I liked it in the summer when its shade would envelop me in the nice cool air. In the fall, the pine needles would drop and I would pick them up and make a fan, a duster or a broom with the pine needles and a stick. In the winter, I would get the pine cones and make a wreath. In the spring, I would get a dead branch that had fallen and whittle it and make a flimsy cane and play with it for maybe a minute or two before it broke.

This tree brought me peace and happiness. One day, I was visiting my grandparents, Gaga and Papa, who live right up the hill from my aunt Kari, uncle Peter and their kids, Will (ten), Alice (eight) and Sarah (five). I can walk from one house to the other house in less than five minutes. Since they live in the country, it's nice to have neighbors who are relatives. The last day that I was staying there at Gaga and Papa's house there was a tremendous thunderstorm.

It all started when my sister Jean and I were playing on the computer. All of a sudden, I saw two things happen at the same time. I was playing a really easy game called Math Wasters. I was on the last level and I was almost going to get my best score, and all of a sudden—ZAP!—the computer flashed off and on. The other thing I saw out of the corner of my eye was a big flash of lightning slashing through the sky. It looked almost like a sword with spikes coming down. Right after the lightning struck, the rain fell harder. My sister got scared (I got scared, too).

We told Gaga about it and she said, "Turn off the computer, because the lightning that we saw probably hit something near by."

We turned off the computer and went to play Sorry with my grandparents next to the back door. When I was setting the game's blue figures up, Will, Alice and Sarah ran in the back door and screamed, "Our house is on fire!"

Those are the scariest words.

After hearing that no one was hurt, we sat down in the study where we could see the smoke and watch the driveway safely. We saw my Mom driving up the driveway in a reckless state. She was crying and keeping an eye on the smoke rising from the tops of the trees. Jean and I ran to see her and tell her no one was hurt. After she heard that the family was safe, she stopped crying. She sighed and said that that is the important part. Jean and I told Mom to come in. That was when it all hit the kids and we came out of shock and started sobbing our heads off (especially me). Just thinking of that house made me cry.

After the fire was out we heard what had happened. The lovely pine tree that was next to the garage had been struck by lightning (the same bolt of lightning that Jean and I had seen on the computer). The tree caught fire and the fire spread to the house. That evening we went into the house and it was all black with the soot and ash. It was really strange to see the house that I had been in so many times, partly gone. It still smelled like smoke and the remaining carpet on the floor was soaked. There was a pile of belongings the fire fighters had put under a piece of black rubber in the middle of the living room floor so they wouldn't get wet. The blackened windows were streaked with water from the fire hoses giving the rooms an eerie tint.

The tree had been burned; so they had to cut it down. Now, I go down to see the house, and all I see are the black house and the stump where the tree used to be.

Dead Tree
by Michael Earley

Two months ago, my friend Steve asked me if I would help him put up his bird feeder. I said, "Sure," and asked him what I had to do. "Well you have to put a screw with string on it in one of the holes in that tall tree." Then he asked me when I wanted to go put it up. I said, "Right now would be fine." So Steve, my Dad and I went to get the ladder.

The tree was old and dead and had no branches. A family of Redheaded Woodpeckers lived in it. The tree was only half there, yet it was almost as big as Steve's three-story house. Dad leaned the ladder up against the tree. I started to climb; my legs were shaking. I looked down when I was five steps up and it looked much farther than when I was down there looking up. I still had a long way to go. I kept climbing. I started to look for a hole in the tree that was the right size for the screw. I only found holes too big or too small. I went farther up. When I was almost all the way up, I found a hole that was almost perfect, but it was a little too big. I went up more and found one that was small, but I jammed in the screw and tightened it with a screwdriver. Then I started down. The ladder was creaking, but it did not fall.

We still had to attach the string to the tree and the deck and put the bird feeder on the string between the tree and the deck, so that the squirrels could not get to it. Amazingly enough, they got the bird seed by hooking their tails to the string and hanging over to get the seeds. And it's been fun to watch the squirrels do acrobatics.

The Giving Tree Report
by Dustin Chambers

On the front corner of our yard we have the most beautiful, biggest dogwood tree in all of Morningside, or at least that's what everyone says that stops by in their car to look at it.

It has pink buds and the biggest trunk. I used to climb it, but now that it is dying it doesn't have any leaves for shade. It doesn't feel like a fort anymore, because everyone can see me. I feel like I have more protection when no one can see me.

We have a swing that is a black rubber horse. It is made out of tire pieces but we found a wasp's nest in the head of the horse. So now we can't swing on it.

Another reason I don't like to climb the tree is that it doesn't have all the limbs that I used to love to climb. They were dead and rotten so we had to cut them off. But all I know is that that tree has been a part of every birthday party my sister and I have ever had. I know it has had a long life because the arborist who lived next door came over and said that it was the biggest, oldest dogwood tree he had ever seen.

Seasons

by Emily Grossniklaus

My tree is probably not like anyone else's tree. My tree is a beautiful oak tree. Well, that's what I think, anyway. It's in my back yard, sort of set away from the house. Most of its branches are very high up, so it's almost impossible to climb.

It is so special to me because it reminds me of my life. When I see it, I think of all the choices I have to make, and of all the snarls and bumps along the way. I shake the tree sometimes, reminding myself of how fragile life is. I love to throw my arms around the tree. This reminds me of all my family and friends, and how much they love me.

Every morning when I wake up, I see my wonderful tree. It's up with me. As new seasons come, they come with the tree. When fairies paint the tree's leaves, I know winter is coming soon. My beautiful tree has three main trunks and its long, swaying arms filter sunlight into my bedroom. I can tell what direction the wind is blowing from the movement of those shady branches. Sometimes it seems like my tree is me. It seems happy when I'm cheerful.

Over the summer, I read a book called *The Gammage Cup*. In the story, each family has a tree planted in their front yard, bearing the name of "family tree." I think my oak tree would be our family's tree, even though it's in the backyard. I call the oak tree *my* tree, though really it's not. It just seems like it's my tree, because I'm the only one in our family to sit between its roots, enjoying the peace and quiet.

When you sit on my bed, and let your imagination run wild, you are suddenly in a tree house.

The sour, apple-green leaves spread a yellowish glow on the carpet. The beautiful dusk sky casts intriguing shadows, and rays of light look like rays from heaven. Even though my tree may not be as beautiful as some, in my eyes it is. In my eyes it's a wonderful tree for me.

The Apple Trees
by Robert Herrig

The first time my brother, Charlie, and I went to Highlands with Ruth and Paul, it snowed and snowed and snowed. The white, sparkling flakes fell hard all night. When I woke up the next morning, the powder was just about taller than me. The snow covered everything, even the trees by the back porch. That was the week of the blizzard of '93. We were snowed in for more days than we had expected.

The next summer, Ruth and Paul invited Charlie and me to go to Highlands and stay at their log cabin, Perseverance. We went the week of July 4th and that was when I noticed that the trees by the back porch were apple trees.

This was my most favorite week of my life. That week we met Alex and Morgan, who were visiting their grandparents who lived right down the road. We also met Knucklehead, the dog, who attacked Charlie and me about five hundred times. Knucklehead was a very strange dog. No one knew where he was from, and he seemed pretty stupid to all of us; so we tried to stay away from him. Ruth and Paul had Dancer that year, probably the meanest horse in the whole state of North Carolina. Dancer was a gorgeous, bright red horse that any horse lover would want to have. Dancer was beautiful and strong, but his attitude did not fit his character, and he wouldn't let us get near him.

The apple tree was the best. We picked the apples that had fallen from it. The tree was big and bulky, and there was always some moss on it. Its bark was like thin, hardened clay, but could give you a nice big scar if your foot slipped while climbing it. The tree was wide at the bottom with its limbs spreading out like an umbrella keeping the rain off a young child.

After the apples fell, we would go pick them off the ground and drop them in a tin bucket. The sound was an annoying thud that would echo through the mountains. When we took the apples to the house, we would make things such as apple pie, apple crisps, apple butter and apple cider. We did not use the rotten ones; so Charlie and I would take them to the creek. Pretending our shirts were baskets, we would carry them and set them on the bridge. Then we would drop them in the water and watch them float like leaves until they went over the waterfall.

This year when we came up for the 4th of July, Charlie, my brother, and Charlie, a college kid who was taking care of the house, made up a game. They would put a bucket in the grass by the fence and throw apples off the back porch and try to get them in the bucket. We would go down into the moist, bright-green grass and pick up as many apples as we could. My brother and I always wanted the most apples to throw. Then we all walked up to the back porch and got ready to throw. When we were set, one of us would shout out, "Go!" Then it was silent, as the apples soared across the sky. Thud, thud, thud as they hit the bucket. Then we picked up another apple. Laughing and not caring where they went, we sent them flying. Sometimes my apple made it and sometimes Charlie's. We would laugh at the sound of the apple hitting the bucket. I not only became good friends with Charlie, but became better friends with the land and the country. We all realized we would never forget this special time and place.

This summer there was a terrible tragedy in Highlands. Ruth and Paul's house and the apple tree burned to the ground. There has been a lot of mourning by those who felt the presence of Perseverance's spirit of happiness. Even though the house and tree are gone, these happy and persevering times will not be destroyed within us.

My Magnolia Tree
by Maisie Richards

My tree is tall and thick. It has been through a hurricane, but not much fell from its branches. My tree is too strong.

One year ago my friend and I buried a treasure. We want someone to find it many years from now. I hope a tractor doesn't before a nice human does. My tree will make sure of that. When I play basketball in my court, I try to shoot from as far away as I can. If my ball touches the leaves of the tree, it almost always goes in. If the ball doesn't touch the leaves, then it almost never goes in.

My tree is a very lucky tree. I remember when I used to play fairies with a friend and we would pretend that my tree was the long leg of a human. The soft leaves of the tree were the sock of the long foot. The trunk was the bare leg. The foot was harmless.

My tree has lost much of its gnarled bark. When I was mad, I would come down the steps, screaming with anger and run to find a stick. Then I would run down the path by the swing and pound the stick against the fragile bark. The bark has grown back now.

I used to play warrior with my sister and fight the tree. The slimmer branches would wave back and forth in a motion that looked as if it was fighting, too. It looked like the leaves were the fingers, clutching a sword. My tree won't really hurt anybody, though.

I would play St. George and the Dragon with my tree. Me and my tree would switch parts, but my tree was better at playing Dragon, because when I hit it, some of the leaves would fly off looking like flaming green fire. The Dragon was harmless, though.

My tree's branches are too far up for me to reach; so I can't climb it. It doesn't matter; it is still playful and beautiful. Under the fresh green leaves are piles of dead branches and brush. Surrounding that is a circle of rocks, piled on top of each other. In the crevasses of the rocks grow moss and small green clumps of monkey grass. The tree's branches reach down as if they are guarding something.

When it rains, the drops fall off the leaves like tears streaming down soft, silky cheeks. When it rains, I know what my tree is guarding. It is a human, guarding its fairy friend. It is a dragon guarding its gold and jewels. A flower guarding its stem. A mushroom guarding a small toad. A mother guarding her child. A cloud guarding the Sun. An army guarding their armor. Mother Nature guarding Life. A tree guarding buried treasure. A tree guarding moss covered rock and monkey grass. A house guarding its owner. My tree guarding me.

Chapter Five

Trees As Companions

You can live for years next door to a big pine tree, honored to have so venerable a neighbor, even when it sheds needles all over your flowers or wakes you, dropping big cones onto your deck at still of night.

—*Denise Levertov*

Cypress
by J. P. Dancing Bear

I am the tall lone cypress
believer of the deeper rhythms
a sentinel of roots and branches
a watcher of clouds and waves
Mother of leaves and cycles
kissing the water and the earth underneath
I am the healer of air
chanting in the cold wind
Stay with me children
climb my length
hum with me
dance my roots
as your parents and grandparents have
Care for me
like I care for you
Sleep in the love and comfort
of my shade
tend to me
that I might live to love
your children
and whisper them the
soft gentle secret ways of nature.

Branches of Life

by Marian Mills-Godfrey

"Get a pet and you'll live longer," says my cat-lover friend, as Madame X, his geriatric cat, sprawls on his lap. He lavishes his hand through her long, white hair and the cat vibrates with appreciation. "New research reveals that people who live alone with a pet will outlive their peers," he continues.

In a letter, my sister writes, "Since you are retired and spend more time home alone, don't you get lonely? Have you thought about adopting a pet? A dog would be a wonderful companion for you to talk to and to hug."

I like my empty nest. I don't want a "live-in" who won't share the rent, who can't pay for health insurance, who's not inclined to help with household chores.

Pets may promote a longer life span, but I believe the same is true for trees. For two decades, I have carried on an affair with a special tree in the park near my apartment building.

We met, my tree and I, on a misty September morning, the day the doctors disconnected my son's life support. At the end of a long jog, blinded by tears mixed with mist, I stumbled off the park path and staggered into a petite, pink crab apple tree, sheltered in a circle of green ash, white pine and silver maple. I wrapped my arms around a sturdy limb, pillowed my head on its stubby skin and sobbed.

A tingling sensation tickled my cheek and swept pain down to my feet. Then a surge of might flowed through my body. For a moment, I felt free from grief and grounded with mother earth. With a powerful sense of peace, I trudged home to do what had to be done.

Ever after, in every season, I end my daily run at the park to hug my tree. Through the branches of the white pine, we watch dawn crawl over the edge of earth and light the sky. I say my morning prayer, "Oh, little tree, petite like me, give me some energy to make it through this day."

Recently, my military daughter launched a long distance campaign to persuade me to adopt a pet. In her latest attack, she sent a clipping from the European edition of *The Stars and Stripes* with these words underlined: "The fact that pets listen and seem to understand but do not question or evaluate may be one of their endearing assets." I often whisper secrets to my tree and, like a mute animal, she responds with silent strength and energy.

Now in our twilight years, our skin is cracked like a crazed porcelain vase. We embrace at eventide, and follow the sun as it sinks to the horizon.

My crab apple suffered several amputations, but according to her surgeon, she will live well into the next century. She continues to grow and reach toward the sunlight and yes, she will outlive me.

Through the years, I paid my respect at pet funerals. I supported friends who mourned and held their hands while Kevorkian vets released the souls of their pets. I remember Eleanor's, Sueann, a protective pug; my neighbor Elizabeth's, Mister, a canary who sang opera; and others too numerous to mention, who were not replaced. When a pet departs this life, does the life expectancy of the owner revert to the status of one who lives alone without a pet?

"Madame X is terminal," my friend says, "I'm digging her final resting place in my backyard."

He plans no replacement. I will add her name to the above list and offer compassionate advice, "Get a tree."

The Weeping Tree
by Kathleen Lohr

When the wild mouths
of first love promise
the willow listens.

The earth tastes of silence
and grey swings creak
on butter-soft porches
phrases sway
then fall like feathers
and the willow listens.

While babies smell of jazz
their cries like small mice
in the jasmine silvered nights
and the lights surrounded by moths
whose wings flutter
uncertain on the edges of black
the willow listens.

Inside bricked rooms
when grampa lays
aside his coffee spoon
because the moon is made
of blue cheese
not green
the willow listens.

Sides are chosen
no matter which
it's the spirit of the thing
and still the willow
with its branches bent

the tips brushing the grass
like loving brooms
listens, listens.

As time is laid aside
like pine cones
that roll on empty roofs
over evening shutters
or morning lace
when the children say
see, see the willow tree
the willow still listens
and weeps.

Communion
by Michael Stephans

Out of the hillside
your perfect symmetry,
alone and rising;

up thorny grade,
with weight of two lives,
I come to you.

Bone and bark,
wine and rainwater,
arm and branch,

We lean into the wind
together, our song—
the coming of winter,

its chorus grown distant;
the retreat of sunlight,
as we commune in

the litany of lost days.
The traffic of songbirds,
long since flown away

to other worlds where
other graying men come to talk
with other oaks and redwoods,

their branches barren,
their songs eternal.

Mimosa

by Jean Lengwin

As winter turned to spring in 1983, when the days began to grow longer and periods of sunshine came more often, we moved the little Birch tree from the area where the new walkway would soon be. We dug around wide and deep, as carefully as we could. We dug a hole of generous proportions in front of our kitchen window to accommodate his vigorously growing roots, then gently carried him to his new site and planted him with care. Day by day I kept a watchful eye.

As the days passed, it wasn't looking good for our young Birch. He wasn't bursting forth with green as the other trees were in their response to spring. Maybe the move had been a setback. Maybe it needed a little extra time. But as time went on, we knew the Birch was a goner. Unceremoniously, my husband pulled the little guy up and tossed him on the burn pile. Though he wasn't yet much of a tree, the spot he vacated looked naked without him.

I drove into town to visit the nursery. I had another Birch in mind, but I kept getting drawn back to a Mimosa. Nothing more than a stick. A two-year-old, the lady said. A two-year-old stick with a slight graceful curve in a gallon container. I paid twenty-nine dollars for what she described as a slow-growing tree that would eventually offer an umbrella of shade during the hot months of the year.

I'm not sure what the lady meant by slow-growing, because this tree has been anything but. As soon as we got the tree out of that small can and into the ground, she started growing and has never stopped. She grew higher and sent out graceful branches. By the time she was five or six, she was in our faces—literally. Her branches drooped into the walkway to our front door; so we had to duck or walk around them. We had her pruned, then pruned some more. She just kept growing. By ten, she was bigger than any of the old Mimosa trees in town by a long shot. The umbrella of shade for my kitchen window now shades most of the front of the house as her handle grows taller each year.

Her lush, green canopy is a sight to behold. When the display of delicate pink, fragrant flowers beckon the humming birds, we know what a gift this tree has been.

I've tried talking to her. "Slow down, Mim," I say. "You're not an Oak. You don't need to grow so big. You've grown taller than our house and as wide as the sky. Enough already, before you invade the foundation and the septic." I hate to even think of what would happen then.

At the end of each summer as fall breezes and cold nights rob her of her beauty, her faded flowers and leaves rain down to litter all beneath her. With the first good rain, the gutters become packed and water spills over at the jams. Fall cleanup is a monumental chore involving my husband, one long ladder and a long handled rake for the roof. On the ground, I man another rake, large scoop shovel and trailer attached to a riding lawn tractor. It's a lot of work keeping up with her, now that she's a teenager.

We shaped and guided her during her adolescence. She's managed to get her head over the rooftop and has sown her wild oats, as is evidenced by young Mimosas sprouting up here and there on our ten acres. Yet, we know her roots are firmly planted. At seventeen, she's a beauty—more than a little taller than most of her kind, but graceful and slender and nothing less than magnificent.

My Life Long Love Affair With a Tree
by Mary Reiter

(1943) As I step over and between the barbed wire fence, a lone cow with big brown eyes gazes woefully at me. "What are you doing? This is my pasture!" I sit down beneath an ancient and gnarled oak tree, of which there are many. I hear its murmuring voice. The squirrels scold me. I dream. I muse..."Is there another baby on the way? Will this awful war ever be over?" The tree rustles its solace.

(1948) The cows are gone, the gamboling horses are gone, the fence is gone. My own tree remains. A college buys all the land, all the trees. My tree is still there.

(1952) Beneath it, my sons and dogs play cowboy and Indians, build forts, skip stones, fall in the pond, play at war. A wise village council buys all the land for $60,000. A true bargain, with one contingency: It must be named Augsburg Park.

(1958) My daughters play in the park, ride bikes, slide down the snow hills. We picnic under my tree.

(1965) The years pass. I sit watching my grandchildren at the Tot Lot, still shaded by my tree.

(1995) Time again passes. I watch my delighted great-grandson on the swing under my tree.

(1998) Now a prayer of Thanksgiving for this beloved place and tree so dear to my heart. So near to my home. A few leaves fall near me. I believe my tree has heard. It holds out its sheltering branches for me and for those who may follow.

The Magnolia Tree and Me
by Dorothy K. Fletcher

Ever since I have moved into my house ten years ago, I have had this running battle—a love/hate relationship—with an enormous, but beautiful magnolia tree that grows in my backyard. It is true that it is a magnificent tree, towering at least three stories into the sky. Its giant canopy provides shade that is sweet and cool, but this magnificent tree makes me absolutely crazy. It sheds constantly—gigantic, slick, brown leaves that are hard to rake and take forever to decompose.

Not that I am opposed to deciduous trees, mind you. I love maples which shed their leaves in the fall, and I love live oak trees that lose their leaves in the spring, but they have the courtesy to lose their leaves all at once and are done with it. Not my magnolia tree. I have had to do my very best to love my magnolia, because I am constantly picking up after it. All year round, in the cold and in the heat, in wind and rain—leaves come down in a dizzying array.

There are times when I actually feel like some kind of cosmic joke is being played on me. No sooner do I have the yard raked than a gust of wind litters my yard with 50 to 100 leaves. No sooner than the lawn mower is tidied away in the shed and I turn to admire my handiwork—a fistful of envelope-sized leaves are floating gently down to mock me.

I have tried all manner of tricks to keep up with the leaves. Once, I tried to compost them, but they apparently have the half-life of uranium. I then decided to scoop them into plastic and paper bags which I would leave lying about in strategic positions. I even tried just picking the leaves up with my bare hands, as if they were an air-tossed deck of cards. This system worked very well until my 45-year-old back began to complain. Mulching the leaves with the lawn mower seemed to be the answer for a while, until the grass began to look choked by the brown residue that was left behind. After that, I began to bag the lawn mower clippings in that heavy contraption on the back. Mowing with the big bag is a heavy and tiring procedure, and one that I most often practice now. I have tried the nail-on-the-end-of-a-rake-handle trick. This works extremely well, except that a nail can only accommodate so many skewered leaves and must be emptied often. This procedure is only good for less than 100 leaves, because more leaves would require as much time as mowing would.

One might wonder why I just don't have the tree cut down and hauled away. I almost did once, when my cat, Jones, climbed to the top and promptly fell to earth with a great thud. The poor cat had to be placed in the "intensive cage unit" at the vet's until we were sure he would survive. Later, as I considered removing the tree, it occurred to me that my cat's accident was not the fault of the tree; so the magnolia won a reprieve.

I have to admit that the tree is a magnificent being, though. I am impressed by its size and by the peaceful atmosphere that it creates under its branches. Many of my potted plants have found a good home at its feet. Many a summer afternoon I find myself under its protective shelter reading my books. *Jurassic Park* was all the more enjoyable when I could look over at the brontosaurus leg-sized magnolia trunk and get into the spirit of the novel. Here, too, novels with Florida settings like *Sugar Cage* by Connie May Fowler or *The Yearling* by Marjorie Kinnan Rawlings are all the more real.

I have finally made peace with this tree mostly by surrendering to its nature and letting it do what it must. I try not to be too grouchy when I have to rake again and again or when I have to spear the errant leaves with my homemade skewer. I look at it as my karma to be a leaf-raker forever, just as Sisyphus is an eternal rock-roller. Besides, it serves no useful purpose to fight it.

As a result, I now sense that the tree may have compromised with me just a little. It seems that there was one whole week in December of 1995 that no leaves fell at all. I took it as a good sign.

Looking Through a Tree
by Jenny Michelle Nadaner

How tall you are
Your branches hover
Swaying, dancing to
The sounds of wind

Your skin is rough
Coarse and uninviting
Sticky, slippery with sap
Smiling
A promenade of ants
March

Your branches smile
Your sap nurtures
And the branches
Sway gently, bringing
Breeze and hope
To the parched world

You reach out
With open arms
Trying to scratch the
Palm of my hand
Asking for attention
A reason to grow taller

Colorful and energetic
Our branches meet
Engaging in friendship
Lifting me aboard

So I sit there
Upon the coarse
Monstrosity
Tall and powerful
Hidden between the
Nurturing Sap.

Redwood Wedding
by Robin Lopez Lysne

A rock shaped like a heart
inside a tree?

I curl into it
and sit in the deep
drone it makes,

regarding its curves
and resident spiders.
I am at home here.

Other people pass by
which does not change
the music inside the tree.

A child cries in the distance.
Flute notes drift up from the valley.
Rusty bark catches the light.

There is a wedding
going on inside.

Pruning

by Johanna Herrick

I prune my lime tree
under the luminous moon
of early evening.
The citrus smell of the broken leaves
is pungent and wonderful.
I know the cutting will make the tree
stronger and even more beautiful.
It trusts me and responds to the pain,
for already, even the order of shaping
has produced a different mood for us;
the discarded sprigs on the ground
ring the tree like a variegated lime lei,
my offering to this faithful tree,
my promise that things will change
between us.

As I pause in the process,
as I breathe and observe and feel,
I encounter the tree, which
ceases to be an "it" and
transforms itself into Buber's "thou."
In this new, reciprocal relationship,
we move toward holiness,
the tree and I,
As I whisper, "You, tree."

A Tree By the Path
by David Ray

—after Tagore

They wondered why I stood and gazed
so long at that tree.

But I knew they would scorn me
if I told them the reason—

that I knew I had never before
been worthy of that tree.

To them such trees are common
and of no value. They'd never

be caught gazing or chanting
or wishing to be worthy,

passing the entrance test of benignity.

My Old Chestnut Tree
by Chuck Dobbs

When I was a kid growing up in Buffalo, New York, we had a small park about a block from my house. Standing in the middle of this park was a huge, old chestnut tree. Some of its roots stuck up out of the ground. When I was very young, I used to believe they were mountains when I played with my toy soldiers. It was so big around that four of my friends and I could hold hands and just reach around its trunk. The branches seemed to touch the sky, and we used to dare each other to climb up to the top, but none of us ever did.

During the summer, its green leaves protected us from the sun, and we marveled at the colors it would turn in the fall. During the summer we used to throw sticks up into the branches to see how many chestnuts we could knock down. We never did anything with the chestnuts, but put them into grocery bags and competed to see how many we could get by the end of the summer. It always seemed as though my best friend, Shawn, had at least twice as many bags as I did. Usually, before the summer's end, our moms got tired of seeing all these chestnuts lying around and would toss our hard-earned bounty unceremoniously into the trash. From our reactions, you would think they had thrown out bags of gold, but it was soon forgotten as our next youthful project came about.

We had a rope swing tied to its lowest branch in the summers and would spend hours playing Tarzan, Zorro, James Bond, or whatever superhero we were into at the time. It was always Shawn, the bravest of the group, who would climb the eight feet into the air to attach the rope. Once, on a dare, Shawn boosted me up to the branch. I never was good with heights, but I had been dared and I was feeling a bit braver than usual. I got up there and discovered that I couldn't get down. After Shawn quit laughing, he took off in the direction of home. I figured he left me to die on that branch, but a couple of minutes later here he came on his bike, making siren noises, carrying a ladder. We laughed for hours about that.

When I was 16, I had a horrible crush on my friend's sister, Carol. She was petite, blond, and beautiful. I never could get up the nerve to ask her out. When Shawn told me that he wanted to ask Carol out, I was devastated, but Shawn was like my brother; so I acted as go-between for the two. I told Carol that Shawn liked her, Carol told me she liked Shawn, passing messages between the two until they got up the nerve to talk to each other directly. Each message was like an ice pick in my heart, but I was doing it for two people whom I loved. I felt like Cyrano de Bergerac without the happy ending. I was with them for that first kiss, which happened right under the tree. I felt angry and betrayed, even though I helped it happen. They started home and I stayed behind, not wanting to interfere with their budding romance, and not really feeling like being with either of them at that moment. Feeling like it was the only friend I had, I sat under my tree for a long time, letting the anger build. Finally, feeling like I would burst if I didn't do something, I stood up and started hitting my tree. Tears in my eyes, I hit it till my knuckles looked like hamburgers. Exhausted, I sat down, my back leaning against his trunk. Never once did my tree complain.

I moved out west after I got married and lost touch with most of my childhood friends, as many of us do. Last I heard, Dempster was a bigwig in some international company and Shawn an engineer in Watertown, New York. I have no idea what became of the others. I do think of my tree once in a while, but only as comparisons with other trees I see. "Oh, that one isn't as tall as my tree" or "my tree spread out much better than that one." But it wasn't as much in my thoughts as my other friends.

A few years back, I flew home for my grandparents' funeral. After the funeral, I was walking around the old neighborhood, feeling a bit sad. So much had changed in the long years I had been away. The corner mom and pop store where we used to get candy was gone, the proprietor long dead. The bank where my grandpa took me to open my first savings account was now a laundromat, all my friends were gone to different parts of the world, the old house seemed so small, and I remembered the quote that said, "You can't go home again." I was just kind of following my feet, when I looked up and saw my tree. I walked up to it and put my hand on its trunk. The bark was just as I remembered, that strange combination of roughness and smoothness. I looked up and it was even taller than I remembered, and looked like it would take a few more friends to reach around its trunk. I started remembering Shawn and all my other friends and the good times we had with our tree. I sat down with my back against it, as we had done so many times before, and I could almost hear them calling to me to play baseball. I remembered all the times we sat in its shade, just like I was doing now, just talking about everything and nothing. I looked up and saw a chestnut hanging off a branch. I picked up a nearby stick and hit it the first time, sending it falling to the ground at my feet. With a smile on my face, I picked up the chestnut, turned around and placed my hand on its rough bark one more time, silently thanking it for still being there, then started home, a little lighter in the heart than when I came.

My Personal Old Growth
by George Baggett

I have always claimed not to be a "tree hugging" environmentalist. My concerns have been more associated with ozone
depletion, ozone smog, point sources, PCBs, dioxins, endocrine
disruption, chromosomal aberration, vinyl chloride, and... When
they tore down trees on the Plaza (KCMO shopper's paradise) to
make room for flush creek "improvements," I thought, "No big
deal." It was not an old-growth forest; the trees were landscaping.
Look at the resulting flood control causeway (a static pond with
dead fish floating and bacteria climbing the edge threatening to
crawl the streets and sidewalks of the Plaza) and just think of what
we gained for the loss of a few fifty-year-old elm trees.

No, I am not a tree hugger, but I do have a story about a tree.
You see, I have my personal old-growth forest. Actually, it is an old-
growth tree. My tree is a white oak, strategically located six inches
from my garage. It stands a good ninety feet tall, the trunk is
roughly four feet in diameter for the first forty feet of the tree. And,
to be honest, there is some question of who owns who. There is
also a question of whether the garage or the tree was there first.
The garage is on the historic register with the Landmarks
Commission. My guess is that the tree was there first, and the guy
who built the garage thought that he would be long dead before
the tree started causing any problem for the garage. He was right.
The tree provides plenty of shade in the summer, drops a good six
inches of debris on the garage and my yard every year, and its root
system has been lifting one corner of the garage ever since the
builder's funeral in 1950.

To gain a full appreciation of my old-growth tree, one must
look at the site. It is near a park in downtown Kansas City,
Missouri, where the tree has many relatives. My property is forty
by a hundred-and-twenty feet and the six-by-twenty-foot garage is
located at the northeast corner of the lot. The tree is on the west
side of the garage. At times, I have seen over six inches of oak

leaves covering my yard. Backyard composting to manage over forty bags of leaves and two fifty-five gallon containers of acorns is out of the question. Blessed are the winds of fall that let my neighbors share in the burden. Squirrels love the tree, not only for the ample food that it provides, but also for the access to my roof and soffits, where they build nests and bore into my attic.

One year after a bumper crop of acorns, I felt sorry for the squirrels digging up my yard to corner the market on acorns. After burying a hundred acorns each, they all had this dazed look on their faces; so I filled two fifty-five gallon containers and stored them in my garage. My thought was that they might feel less compelled to procreate if there was a shortage of acorns, but it was a bumper year for squirrels as well.

In February, with six inches of snow on the ground, I pulled one of the containers into the yard and poured the acorns into a pyramid about two feet tall. To my surprise, it took a couple days for the squirrels to notice them. They walked by them, probably not recognizing them for acorns. Finally, one squirrel noticed. He climbed to the top of the pile like king-of-the-mountain and looked around to see if any others had noticed his find. Then he started taking them one at a time and burying them in the snow. Instead of getting help, he started storing them on limbs of the tree, on the roof of the garage, and anywhere he thought others might not find them.

Exhausted from his hoarding, he sat on the pile eating them as fast as he could. When others noticed, he was like a benevolent dictator with some, and protector of the home front with others. An existential mood took over in the end. He just stood back and watched the carnage as younger squirrels ate them on the spot, leaving the shells and caps commingled with the fresh meated acorns. After a while, it took some sorting to find a good acorn to eat. The second barrel of acorns went away slower, and no one attempted ownership or control.

A careful look at my oak tree and one will notice that it leans about five degrees off the vertical, as if it attempted to avoid contact with the garage. It looks like it is ready to fall over in a good wind, yet I have seen it take winds of over fifty miles-per-hour.

The root system must be as large as the tree. When I had it trimmed a few years back, one of the trimmers fell in love with the tree (a real "tree hugger tree trimmer"). In his opinion, the tree is in no danger of falling any time in the near future. Not that I wish the tree any harm, but I have flirted with the revolutionary thought of having a two-car-garage. If the tree fell, it would likely take the garage with it and open a space large enough to have that spacious garage.

My father lived in the house for almost forty-five years and had to move to Leawood, Kansas, to have a two-car-garage. My fate may be the same.

Decision

by Grace Butcher

The tree knew, I think. It did the best it could, did what it had to do under the circumstances.

Primitive people endowed all of nature with a soul, every object with a spirit to be spoken to, apologized to, praised, asked for advice. Scientists have measured the force fields of living things. The power unleashed by nature makes all of our mightiest weapons seem puny. And although we know what a thunderstorm is, for instance, we don't know why. That is, we don't know why all these elements "decide" to come together at that time, that place. Oh, we can say that the temperature was thus and the humidity so; that the winds come from here and the clouds from there—but why? And for every answer there's yet another "why" until eventually there is no answer except in mystical terms.

The willow tree didn't seem especially mystical. My folks planted it when I was about fourteen. Typical of its kind, it grew very fast, but I don't remember much about its adolescence which seemed, more or less, to correspond with my own. By the time I was an adult, so was the tree.

It seemed a marvelous combination of masculine and feminine: its massive, muscular branches perfect for climbing, hugging and sitting on. Its long, filmy green skirt reached to the ground and made a little private place inside its lacy screen. To sit in there, leaning against the huge, comforting trunk at twilight was to see the slender leaves turn to black wings against the darkening blue-black of the evening sky. In fall, its long, green tendril-like branches seemed covered with yellow candle flames burning in the brilliance of October.

My refuge was like a green and golden cage that didn't so much keep me in, but kept the world out. Even as an adult, I would climb the tree for that childlike joy in leaving the earth under my own power, and the delightful sense of secrecy and superiority I felt when my family would walk into the yard not knowing I was there, nearly invisible, godlike, surveying the world below.

The tree appears so often in my poetry that I still refer to a time called my "willow tree phase." When the tree was at its peak of beauty and maturity, I likened myself to it in every way I could. My hair, arms and body made metaphors of its roots, its graceful strength. It seemed to fill the backyard and somehow manage to wrap around the corner of the house to appear in both of my bedroom windows, one on the west wall, the other on the north.

I remember one sunny day years ago going into that room to do some chore or other and being overwhelmed by the beauty of what I saw. The wind was blowing, and the delicate branches of the willow filled both windows with a surging, flowing sea of gleaming green. It was as if I were looking out into some magical underwater scene, the whole room submerged in a surging emerald ocean. I laid down on the bed and drifted away in the green glow. The peacefulness of that enchanted hour will always be with me.

So the years went by, but while the maples and oaks and evergreens surrounding my old farmhouse seemed to just keep imperceptibly growing, the willow did not. And on one still summer night, my son and I heard a strange, loud noise in the yard and ran out to see what had happened. A large branch from the willow had simply broken off, all its still-growing twigs and shoots now jammed, broken, into the ground. Above, the jagged break of the eight-inch limb hung by shreds to the tree showing us its half-rotted center.

I was dismayed. The tree had looked raggedy for some time, but I hadn't wanted to notice, I guess. Now I couldn't trust it any more and no longer sat under it, nor could I allow friends or family to do so either. I thought vaguely of calling somebody to come and trim it, doctor it, take care of it. But somehow I didn't think it would do any good; the tree was slowly dying year after year. "Maybe I should have it taken down," I said to my son one day, and he agreed that maybe I should. It was too close to the house and garage for us to risk cutting it down ourselves; besides, we didn't own the proper equipment to tackle such a huge tree.

Somehow the thought of taking it down didn't seem right. My parents, now dead, had planted it. I had grown up with it, written about it, sat under it, talked to it. Take it down? No. Like the old white hens who no longer laid eggs but still wandered the back yard in their retirement, it, too, could stay there as long as it wanted. It had given me too much pleasure for me to hire some kind of assassin to come and strike it dead.

But year by year, more and more of the tree died. Its long, green skirts had not touched the ground for a long time, and in fact didn't even exist any longer. More branches broke and fell in strong winds. I tried not to see how much of it was dead. Finally, I called a local landscaper to come and give me an estimate for cutting it down; it was not a safe tree to have any longer. For some reason he never came, and secretly relieved, I didn't call again.

A year or so later, though, I read about a young boy who had been on his paper route in a wind storm when the dead top of an old maple tree came crashing down and killed him. I could no longer ignore the potential tragedy in my own backyard. How long would it be before my negligence would cause someone to get hurt? I made another phone call this time making certain the man would come to give me an estimate for having my beloved willow tree cut down and hauled away.

He came when I was not at home and left a note in the door for me with the price for the job. It was a lot of money, but with the tree so close to the house and all—well, I called him and said, "OK. Come as soon as you can." I felt sad and uneasy all the rest of the evening, almost as if I had arranged to have an old and faithful dog put to sleep.

The wind was rising as I went up to bed about midnight taking along a book to read. My century old farmhouse creaked like an ancient ship under sails riding out the windstorms. But something was wrong; I sat in bed with my book unread on my lap feeling some kind of terrible pressure building up all around me. I thought of the willow tree so close outside my bedroom window and of the huge wind rocking it to its weary roots.

I felt a tension and anxiety that grew by the minute as the wind roared, slamming itself against my house. Suddenly, from outside came a huge, dark, mysterious, shuddering noise that I had never heard before. Then the sound of breaking glass from the garage. I knew what had happened. I knew. I jumped up and threw on my clothes, calling to my son, "I think the willow tree has fallen!" And we ran outside into the wild buffeting of the wind.

There, right by the corner of the house as the wind whipped our hair and clothes around, we saw something enormous and incredibly shaped, darker than the night. The faint light from the back porch splashed on the massive trunk of the willow tree lying in the small space between the house and the garage. Its branches seemed to be all over the sides of both buildings. The alarm bell on my garage was clanging wildly from the broken window in the small back door, but that was all the damage I could see.

The tiny space that tree had put itself into! Only a narrow sidewalk, an edge of flowers, and a row of bushes separated the house and garage. Yet that giant tree had somehow placed itself in that space, arranging its branches, it seemed, so as to do the least amount of damage. It had pulled a small section of gutter loose from the garage and just caught the downspout on the house, pulling that off. One huge branch rested tightly against a downstairs window but had not broken it. One shutter was slightly dented and three panels of siding scratched, and that was all. I was stunned to think that the tree had done the best it could to fall without hurting anything too much.

We went back into the house and my son went up to bed again. But I sat downstairs in the dark living room and cried. "It knew. It knew," I said aloud over and over as the wind diminished and the night grew still. The tree knew that I had that very night finally decided that it must die. It also knew how much I loved it (if such a feeling may exist between two such different species) and how hard that decision had been to make. But it didn't want to be killed, I reasoned as I sat in the dark, listening to the wind which no longer had any power to bother me as it moved on to other tasks. The willow tree had made an arrangement with the wind and taken itself down. It did it the best possible way it knew how, squeezing itself into the only space available for it. A foot to the left or right would have caused extensive damage to the house or garage. It did the best it could.

And last of all, if the man had come to cut it down, a huge and ugly stump would have been left as a reminder of my painful decision. But the tree broke itself off under the ground as it fell, so that once it was cut up and hauled away, there was nothing left at all— only a slight mound of earth, to show where it had been.

All the windstorms it had survived—including an 80 mph

blizzard the previous winter—had not put it down. Only when it somehow knew that after many years of talking about it, I had finally decided on that very night to have it cut down. Only then did it behave in the way that trees and animals and rocks and rivers must have always behaved for those primitive people who believed in such things. It took matters into its own hands.

I sat there in the dark, remembering my parents who had planted the tree, my teenage confidences whispered in the safe embrace of its dark and massive arms, remembering my sons playing under it, remembering that mystical green room floating in the ocean of its branches. That it now lay grotesquely on the ground outside seemed like a bad dream. I was not eager for morning to come when I would have to see that awful horizontal finality, that fatal change of form, by daylight.

At the same time I felt a surge of something like gratitude, awe, respect and relief all mixed together. There had always been something very special about that tree, and the way it chose to die was as special as the way it had lived. Its time had come, and it knew. It did the best it could.

Learning From Trees
by Grace Butcher

If we could,
like the trees,
practice dying,
do it every year
just as something we do—
like going on vacation
or celebrating birthdays,
it would become
as easy a part of us
as our hair or clothing.

Someone would show us how
to lie down and fade away
as if in deepest meditation,
and we would learn
about the fine dark emptiness,
both knowing it and not knowing it,
and coming back would be irrelevant.

Whatever it is the trees know
when they stand undone,
surprisingly intricate,
we need to know also
so we can allow
that last thing
to happen to us
as if it were only
an ordinary thing.

Leaves and lives
falling away,
the spirit, complex,
waiting in the fine darkness
to learn which way
it will go.

Chapter Six

Trees In Memoriam

The greatest wonder is that we can see
these trees and not wonder more.
—*Ralph Waldo Emerson*,
from a conversation with John Muir

The Tree of Life
by Warren D. Jacobs

I am in love with a tree. We were never formally introduced, but I suspect that God had a guiding Hand in the initiation of our relationship. In 1970, I received notice from Washington that I would not be able to complete my psychiatric residency, because I was being drafted into the U.S. Army. I obtained an assignment at Fort Benning, in a place unknown to me at the time called Columbus, Georgia. The military induction precipitated a grave crisis in my marriage, and in the late summer of 1971, I found myself leaving Chicago and driving south on the Dan Ryan Expressway in my 1970 baby-blue Dodge van, which was stripped to the essentials with a rug in the back for stretching and sleeping. My wife and two-year-old daughter stayed in Chicago, and I was alone.

As the city of my birth disappeared behind me on that unbearably hot summer's day, I harmonized with John Denver as he sang about country roads. My heart filled with anticipation and excitement, while at the same time, a gnawing sense of sadness and fear began to grow in an even deeper part of my belly. My state of being mirrored what I saw through my windshield as I rocketed down the highway. There, before me, the open road stretched out seductive arms, while the massive steel mills of Gary, Indiana, belched destruction with fire and black smoke. I had never been south of Gary, Indiana, but now, here I was, heading into my unknown future.

As the mid-West landscape shifted from Indiana's flatness to the rolling green of Kentucky and, finally, to the shelter of Tennessee's peaks and valleys, I entered the Cumberland Mountain range near Chattanooga. Consulting my map, I noticed a large green area in the eastern corner of Tennessee called the Great Smoky Mountains National Park. Having grown up in Chicago, which boasts of a street named Ridge Avenue which is, perhaps, all of twenty feet above sea level, the mountains were electrifying. In addition, when I was eighteen, I had spent a year in Israel on a youth leadership course. Some of my fondest memories include climbing Masada in the pre-dawn darkness and watching the sunrise over the Dead Sea, as well as ascending Mount Tabor in the early-morning fog and gazing down upon the fertile valleys of the Lower Galilee. I have always felt a sense of majesty, peace and holiness in the mountains. So I decided to take a detour on I-75 east to the Park instead of directly south to Atlanta and Columbus.

Passing through Knoxville, Pigeon Forge and Gatlinburg, I eased into the sanctuary of the Smokies. No city horns blared, no billboards exhorted me to "see Rock City" or encouraged me to "eat this," "drink or smoke that" or "lodge or shop here." Rather, I was greeted by sunshine, shadows, a soft, warm breeze on my face, rustling leaves of red, yellow, purple at the road's edge, and green —miles and miles of green. I was heady with summer as I drove down the winding road, and my tension and fear began to disappear with every breath. I decided to spend the night at the campground adjoining Cades Cove.

The next day, I entered the Cove and immediately was drawn into its sheltering beauty—pastures filled with trees that were supported by a sea of waving, deep grass, safely nestled within the surrounding mountains. As I traveled along the narrow, paved road, I wanted to stop my van and rush headlong into a pasture, but the rusty barbed-wire fence was too intimidating. I could only wind down the road, losing myself in the beauty of the landscape.

At one point, the road curved sharply to the left, and I was momentarily distracted. When I looked up, I saw her. I was transfixed. She was in magnificent late summer bloom—a large maple tree with a full crown of foliage standing proudly near the road on a grassy rise. She overlooked a broad, rich meadow, and was framed in the distance by the palpable softness and ancient solidity of the rolling hills. I felt as if her limbs were reaching out to me with beckoning warmth as she enfolded me and tenderly whispered that I would be "all right." Suddenly, a wave of peace and comfort unknown to me for months dissolved any remaining fear and isolation. I pulled to the side of the road, closed my eyes, and imagined King David sitting under the tree playing a flute, guarding his flock in the field below. At that moment, I was filled with an overwhelming sense of awe, safety, and well-being. I was not and would not be alone.

Through the years since our initial encounter, I often returned to my tree during times of pain and joy, always to be embraced, nurtured, and spiritually enriched—a holy place of connection with God. Each visit, I entered the Cove with heightened anticipation, my excitement mounted as I approached the familiar left bend in the road, my joy exploded as I saw her once again. Sleeping bag in tow, I carefully crawled under the barbed-wire fence (meant to separate all but me from the meadow). Walking swiftly through the knee-high grass, I stood beside her, my fingers tenderly restoring our connection as I gently touched her ridged bark. Enfolding her in my arms, I accepted the shelter of her outstretched canopy as she whispered a greeting. I kissed her and told her of my happiness in her presence.

My heart remembers the day when I placed my sleeping bag against her as I stretched along the ground, head resting in a hollow, shaped perfectly for support. I closed my eyes, my breathing slowed, my being relaxed as I gradually became aware of the soft breeze caressing my face, the sweet smell of summer grass, the graceful rustling of leaves, the hypnotic hum of bees, the reflected warmth of the sun-drenched meadow. Suddenly, I was transported into a crack in time, where, but for the briefest instant, "I" no longer existed. For that moment, physical boundaries blurred and I flowed with the Unity of the Universe and the Oneness of God. I was "me" but also not "me." I was tree, grass, bee, wind, sun, mountain, sky and nothing. I felt like Moses standing on sacred ground, overwhelmed with the awareness of the Holy One and simultaneously mindful of my infinitesimally small presence. I drew sustenance from my Tree of Knowledge.

My spirit remembers the day when I sat at the base of my tree and looked skyward beyond her leaves. A slight movement to my left, and there was a hawk, wings unfurled, effortlessly gliding through blue, cloudless space. Mesmerized, I gazed as it floated over the meadow, catching the updrafts, finally becoming a speck over the distant mountains. Before this visit to the Cove, I had been depressed. I had hoped to lift my mood through the healing energy of my tree. Watching the hawk, I realized that my depression could be eased by "catching the updrafts." If I searched for life's positive forces, I, too, would soar. I drew strength from my Tree of Healing Wisdom.

My soul remembers the day when I had finished meditating

under my tree and was reluctantly walking to the car, parked just beyond the wire fence. As I approached, I glanced mindlessly at the windshield and saw the reflection of a rainbow. I was puzzled. It hadn't rained. I looked up at the sky, and directly above me between the clouds was a slice of rainbow. In awe, I watched as it quickly vanished. I knew, *I knew*, in the depth of my soul, that only I saw that rainbow. God gave us the rainbow as a covenantal sign that the world would never be destroyed. God gave me *my* rainbow as a sign of healing the wounds of my past and as a symbol of trust and faith in the future. I drew hope from my Tree of Life.

After other visits to my maple, and a separation of seven years, I returned to Cades Cove in October, 1996, excited with the knowledge that she would be aglow in her yellow fall coat. This time, I rented an RV camper and was accompanied by my wife, brother-in-law, sister-in-law, and nephew. We arrived at the campground after dark, too late to enter the Cove. My disappointment was tempered by the certainty that I would see my tree the next day. I slept fitfully, partially from excitement, mostly from sharing the narrow bed with my nephew. The new day dawned cloudy, cold and wet. After an interminably long breakfast (my wife and family didn't share my unbounded enthusiasm for my tree), we finally drove into Cades Cove. As we rounded each curve, the others razzed me with good-natured ribbing: "Is that your tree? Is it that one?" No matter. I knew where my tree stood. And when I thought I saw her in the distance, my heart opened in anticipation of receiving the blessing of her presence. Finally, we arrived at the sharp left bend, turned the corner, and I raised my eyes to greet my friend. I saw a clear expanse of blue sky, the meadow below, the rolling mountains in the distance...and a stump. I was stunned, shocked, disoriented. Where my beloved maple had stood sentinel over the meadow, there was a shattered, blackened remnant, a sad, truncated being, reduced to a ten foot tall shadow of former glory. It was as if God had torn a hole in His Universe at that sacred spot.

I stayed with my tree as my family journeyed through the Cove. I stood at her side, numb with sorrow, leaning against her. "I always thought you would be here," I mumbled. "I knew you would outlive me, and that for the rest of my life, I would come and sit beside you and feed my soul. Now what can I do?"

As I stared blankly at the mountains in the distance, a man appeared and began to talk of his love for the tree. He related that every October, he and his family would come to Cades Cove just to see her magnificent yellow foliage. I listened quietly as he told me of her death. In the spring of 1994, she was struck by lightning and was topped by the Park Service in an attempt to save her, but the following winter was harsh, and she did not survive. As he spoke, I could hear sadness and regret. I shared mine with him. This unknown spiritual companion and fellow tree lover also told me that the locals had named the maple "The Wedding Tree," a clear indication of their deep connection and affection. I suddenly became aware of a flash of anger and jealousy, as I thought, "This is my tree. Mine alone! Our relationship is unique and powerful and nobody else has claim to her." But her specialness obviously transcended my selfishness. I realized that I could still maintain our deep bond while sharing and embracing the reality of her having touched other lives.

Following our conversation, I reluctantly moved from the tree and stood silently at the side of the road, as if waiting for direction or a sign to soothe my grief. As if my tree was speaking to me, an inner voice unexpectedly expressed a strong desire to perform *Tikkun Olam*, the Jewish concept of "repairing or restoring the world's wholeness"—healing the tear in the Universe at that spot. But how could I?

Suddenly I saw them. A mother and her young children had come to the tree and the little ones noisily clamored for her to take a picture of them on the stump. They enthusiastically positioned themselves and were photographed for eternity. My heart filled with warmth and joy as I comprehended the truth that even in death, my wonderful, magnificent, sacred maple tree continues to nurture and touch the lives of others, as she has touched mine. I then understood the profound message and wisdom granted me from my Tree of Life—love will heal this tear in the Universe. Love will heal all tears in the Universe.

So I tell her story.

Our Tree
by Marion I. Howe

That grand Old Elm
a grand old lady, that tree
stood through rain,
stood through drought,
stood through sleet
and snow and ice
clinging to her branches.

Let us glory in her
presence
take pictures of
her jeweled branches
before the sun swept
her glory jewels
to heaven.

She gave us shade many
a hot, dry summer
held an umbrella over
the old front porch in rain,
hid for us birds' nests
and squirrels' nests
among her branches
safe haven for them
over many a year,
family friends
for generations.

In days gone by
she gave
the circuses cause to stop
on their way up the street
while the animals

quenched their thirst
at the well that
drew at her feet,
while draft elephants
trumpeted jealous notes
while calliopes
slaked their thirst.

She's a grand old, old tree
and if she could've talked
would've told us all a tale.

This grand old tree
stood supple and tall
when our ancestors
came from Norway
to settle here before
the Indian War.
She listened when the Indians left,
heard their chants when
they came back
and sold melons
door-to-door:
"Merry Christmas
-10 cents."

She stood there when
the hobos came
and left their mark
'cause Grandma
gave them a meal.
Stood when her sons
went off to fight
in the
Spanish American
Cuban American
Hearst American
Hawaiian American
Wars.

Stood there
before World War I
and all the times in between.
She stood there
when our great grandparents
came before the Civil War,
moved to the house next door
and made a paintshop there
right there
beneath her branches.

Stood there
when our parents
changed the paintshop
to a house
and lived there
thick and thin
for onto 53 years.

She stood there
through World War II
stood there proud
when we were wed
and brought
our babies home.
Stood there now
we've been wed
49 years.
She stood there
and our family's grown
and moved away.

But today
alone, I sat
and watched
her die.

They came before
the mailman's rounds
unannounced
and stole her
from us all
in the snarl of
the cutters' saws.

She stood there
as I wept today
in the weeping
from the skies
causing the men
to curse wet wood
and broken chains
as their angry machines
and grunting trucks
stole her piece by piece.

We mourn for her
and times gone by
and grieve that
she was taken,
the paper said,
for better curbs
and higher voltage.

So that's
the goodbye
to a Grand Old Tree
they'd have us give,
hooray for cars
for bigger lightbulbs.

O fools,
oh yes,
you're really
something.

An Elm in the Middle of Our Street and Our Lives
by Larry R. Granger

"You can't miss the house. It faces a tree in the middle of Johnson Avenue. See the tree and you're there." Those were the directions I got from a real estate agent who was offering a small, three-bedroom rambler for sale in the western part of Bloomington, Minnesota, in 1961. That was how I was introduced to a huge elm with a twenty foot girth that was dead center in the middle of the street and had a canopy of spreading branches that shaded parts of four lots. The tree was the deciding factor in choosing this house over a similar and lower-priced house further east in the community.

Our Johnson Avenue Elm was actually four elms which had been planted together to form a marker between two farms many years ago. For the next eighteen years, the tree was an integral part of our family life as three Granger youngsters grew into young adults while the elm played out its last days, much like a grandparent, before succumbing to Dutch Elm disease in 1979. That was the year my father died unexpectedly and our thirteen-year-old, much beloved German Shepherd had to be put away. All three events were sad deaths in the family.

In October of 1961, my wife, our three-year-old daughter and I moved into our house and immediately began hearing about the Elm's reputation. The tree was well-known by airline pilots who used it as a daytime visual guide on their approach to the Minneapolis-Saint Paul Airport. It took only a few days to discover that our Elm was the starting point for drag racing south on Johnson Avenue, for there were no stop signs at the cross streets. When we asked the neighbors if the Elm had ever caused a traffic accident, they just smiled.

"Can I go play by the tree before it gets dark," was the request our daughter made not long after we moved in. Over the next few years, it wasn't necessary for Vicky and her two brothers to ask for permission to play by the tree or meet friends there. The tree and its surrounding island of dirt and weeds had become an extension of our yard and a mini-playground for the pack of kids on Johnson Avenue. During daylight hours of the 1960's, traffic was modest and drivers were generally quite careful as they approached the tree and its young playmates.

The 60's on our street was a time of mostly one working parent, one-car families with stay-at-home moms who watched over the neighborhood kids as they roamed between backyards and our middle-of-the-street playground. Few homes had air conditioning; so young and old spent a lot of time outside, often in the shade of our Elm. After all, we were living in what, until the middle 1950's, had been farm fields in a township just starting to experience suburban growth coming south out of Minneapolis.

The ten families who lived on Johnson Avenue each had their own way of interacting with the big Elm. However, it became my special role, because of working for the City, to be protector and watchdog on what the Bloomington Public Work's Department had in mind for our tree. To the traffic engineer, the tree was a menace that needed to be removed. He had not been around when Farmer Brown sold his farm to a developer on condition that the big Elm remain standing, even if it had to be in the street, as it was when the subdivision was platted. An opportunity to eliminate the so-called "traffic menace" came in 1963 when water and sewer pipes were installed on our street as part of a community-wide program of developing central utilities in response to the nitrate contamination of many individual wells. As the contractor came down Johnson Avenue, a decision was made by someone to put the pipes under the tree rather than take it down. I wish I could take credit for this decision, but I think it involved more expediency rather than an appreciation of nature. The term "tree hugger" had not yet been invented but I think that's what many kids and adults were prepared to do. Thus, 1963 became the Elm's peak time, in that some roots were cut and the upper foliage began to die off.

With our Elm's future secured for the time being, it meant that the Granger kids and friends could still use it as their playground. Danny from a couple of houses away, who became a civil engineer, could still organize card games in the shade of the tree. Our son, Brian, and his pal, Jim, who both became CPAs, could still carry their Tonka Trucks out to the tree and do their own brand of construction. Adults and children could still park their bikes, buggies, wagons or strollers and join in the play or just get out of the sun.

There was usually something going on out by the tree when I came home for lunch. I would check it out while trying to retrieve a couple of reluctant Granger kids. "What have you been doing?" was my usual question, often getting the proverbial kid answer, "nothing." Other answers included playing hide and seek, chasing each other around the tree, throwing rocks at the squirrels, keeping the Kell and Irwin Avenue kids out of the tree, playing house, jumping out of the tree like Batman and Robin did on TV, hiding "so and so" whose mother said not to play by the tree or "I'll never tell." In wintertime, the games changed depending on the weather. After big snowfalls, city snowplow operators, Ken and Gordy, who lived in the neighborhood, would creatively place piles of snow around the tree. These could then be used for snowforts and mini-sliding hills. Snowballs would suddenly be launched from the snowforts at those who dared to walk down the street, but only if they were smaller than the snowball throwers.

Our tree had other uses for groups and individuals of many ages, and sometimes these uses were a bit unusual. For several years, a Hennepin County Bookmobile would be parked by the tree over lunch time. Apparently, the shade of the tree was to be preferred over the shopping center parking lots where school buses waited for their afternoon runs. Or perhaps the driver wanted to have a distinctive answer to the question of co-workers and family members: "and where did you go today?"

If the early part of the Elm's day belonged to mothers and young kids, then late afternoon and evenings belonged to teenagers, young adults and the "young at heart." The tree provided a perfect hanging-out spot for teenagers on their way home from Jefferson High School. The tree became increasingly available during the day as the pre-schoolers went off to school and school-age kids got caught up in after-school activities like scouts and sports.

There was a different dimension to teenagers hanging out by our tree beginning in the late 60's and lasting up through the tree's last days. Many of the lounging and chatting teens still rode bikes, but clouds of marijuana smoke often drifted out from the assembled group. Our tree had become a "cool" spot for meeting and smoking and many of us adults were clueless about what was going on.

Once the sun went down, cars with a couple of occupants of the opposite sex started parking next to the tree which then took on another role as a miniature "lover's lane." Often this was the sight that greeted me when I returned home from an evening meeting. If I was annoyed or overly tired, I would sometimes park in the street with my headlights focused on the parkers until they left. My wife did not approve of this, for it reminded her of what the police did to us on the River Road in Saint Paul a couple of decades earlier.

I never talked about all that went on around the tree while I was working at the City. It would just give the engineers some additional verbal ammunition to use in making both the real and humorous case for eliminating our tree. As it was, the City Engineer had a running commentary with me about how they would be coming out some dark night and pound copper spikes in the tree which would soon finish it off.

The reality about the Elm being a traffic hazard was that there was only one recorded instance when a car hit the tree head on and an ambulance was required. I was away when this happened and my neighbors had to give me the details. It was more common that near misses occurred as evidenced by pieces of chrome body trim and hubcaps left near the tree, which sometimes had bark scars from an impact. Yet, there were two very different places where our Elm had achieved notoriety as a car masher. When Johnson Avenue kids went to Junior and Senior high school, they would exaggerate the number of cars crashing into the tree, much like a fish story about the big one that got away. A few blocks from the Elm at Andy's Tap, patrons who had to drive south on Johnson Avenue were given warnings to "look out for the tree."

Both adults and kids appreciated the distinctiveness our Elm gave to our block and neighborhood. "I live on the street with the big tree in the middle" is the direction that our daughter, Vicky, now an IRS Agent, and the other sixty kids who grew up on the street could give to their friends and relatives. As the kids got older, they didn't have much direct involvement with the tree but still considered it "cool" to mention that you had a tree in the middle of your street. Now it was the adults who would wander out by our Elm and look it over and chat. One thing we all agreed upon was that when we turned onto Johnson Avenue and saw our tree, we knew we were home.

For me, the Elm was a special symbol of home starting in the 70's when I began traveling the state and frequently arrived home late at night or early in the morning. It was always a reassuring sight to see the tree, even if it was teepeed with toilet paper by students, as happened during homecoming, Halloween and graduation. In the winter, the kids, now mostly teenagers, didn't play in snowforts anymore. Elms were more of a problem than an amusement. Yet, on a frosty or icy morning, our tree was like a shining ice palace that reminded us that we all lived in a special place.

During the busy 1970's, none of us on Johnson Avenue thought our Elm was in danger, even though Dutch Elm Disease was spreading throughout the city and much of the state. The tree didn't look much different than it did in 1963 when the utility pipes disturbed part of its root system. It was still an attraction, as we found out in the mid 70's when a hot air balloon race went directly over Johnson Avenue and the contestants were pointing at our tree. With fewer kids playing by the tree, the squirrels were comfortable living in the upper branches. There were as many as six squirrel nests and several bird nests in the Elm. When the dreaded red circle appeared on our Elm in 1979, there was a collective sigh of "oh, no" that traveled from house to house. There were also some individual and group inspections of the tree by the residents of Johnson Avenue who became resigned to the loss of our landmark. Not everyone was so resigned to the tree going down. Jimmy, who lived half a block away on 108th Street, visited the tree after dark and painted brown paint over the red circle in hopes of confusing the tree-cutting crew.

It took three days to remove our Elm from Johnson Avenue. Our long-time friend, neighborhood symbol, mini-playground, town square and neighborhood nature center was gone. For the Public Works Department, it meant that a diseased tree and traffic menace was gone. Once the Elm had been marked for removal, I received a call from the City Engineer assuring me that the tree was too diseased to save. But, the story of the Elm in the middle of the street does not end in 1979.

In the coming years, traffic began to speed up on Johnson Avenue at all hours of the day. Our family had one cat killed on the street and another injured in the early 1980s. These were the first pet fatalities on our part of Johnson Avenue. The distinctiveness of our neighborhood was forever altered by the loss of our Elm, and it was questionable whether traffic safety was improved.

At our home, the legacy of the Johnson Avenue Elm lives on in a very unexpected way. From the time we moved to our house and lot in 1961, my wife, Roberta, was regularly asking me to plant additional trees and shrubs for shade. If I did not respond in a timely manner, she would do it herself. And so one day, she picked up four Silver Maple seedlings and shoved them into the ground near the garage. Our youngest son, Bruce, who became an attorney, did not approve and regularly ran over them with the lawn mower. They not only survived, but grew rapidly as Silver Maples do, with a juncture about five feet up where the four limbs divided. It was perfect for perching in by squirrels, birds and grandchildren. By the mid-1990's, our oldest grandson was piling up leaves in the crotch of the tree and playing hide and seek. After Halloween, carved pumpkins would often be deposited in the tree for the critters. And in the upper branches, there were three squirrel nests.

Today, I still travel the state and arrive home at all hours. As I turn onto Johnson Avenue, there is no Elm in the middle of the street to greet me, but there is Roberta's large four-limbed Silver Maple at the end of the driveway. I know I am home even though Roberta passed away in the spring of 1999. Farmer Brown's big Elm and now the Silver Maple have anchored our family memories to our block, our community and our place on this earth, a place called home.

Chinese Elm
by Kenneth Pobo

I was a lucky kid in one way in particular. I was rich in trees.
We had two apples, a tulip tree and a cherry tree in our backyard.
But my favorite was a Chinese Elm.

In Illinois, winter clings. The prairie may have been booted out
by buildings and boutiques, but its gray remains, severe and unwel-
coming. Day after day, I'd get ready for school and see the sunless
sky through my bedroom window—one more gray overcoat I'd
have to wear over the woolen one I already wore.

Finally, those first throbbing hints of spring: the break in the
sky, the sun's peek-a-boo over swingsets and garage roofs.

And the Chinese Elm. Year after year, I took hope from the
unfurling of the smallish green leaves. Ours was the tallest tree in
the neighborhood—that made it special. Once all the leaves were
out and the tree got caught by a prairie wind, it swayed and went
into its ballet.

It didn't make a whole lot of sound when the wind overtook it,
just a rhythm of castanets made out of lacy paper. The leaves would
hold on, hold on, while wind wheeled through the tree.

Stillness. That was elegant, too. The tree standing there, the
sun filtering down branch by branch, and me leaning against its
broken spots of shade. Summers I'd take my transistor radio and
listen to WLS or WCFL under its protection.

1971: Tommy James had a hit single with "Draggin' The Line."
I had always adored Tommy. Still do. One of the lyrics referred to
hugging a tree. I decided to put the song to the test. The tree was
my friend, and it deserved a hug. I was 16.

I believe that tree hugged back. No, the trunk didn't grow
secret arms. Yet every season brought a hug, a touch. Every change
in the light, every wave of moonlight rushing the shore of its bark.

Sometimes I wonder why people give each other gifts, especially things made in factories and sold in stores. Those things,
perhaps well-intended by the giver, feel cold, devoid of anyone's

hands. Keats says that the poetry of earth is never dead. Earth gives, without attention to human holidays. It gives, because its poetry is spontaneous and wild.

The Chinese Elm hurricaned us with leaves in the fall. My father and I would rake them into piles that I would jump in. Sometimes the neighborhood kids and I would add the tree's leaves to others collected from various trees and make a fire. Into the smolder would go potatoes wrapped in tinfoil. I've been to some nifty restaurants, but have never had better potatoes.

It was saddening to see the leaves go. But it was also a special time when I could look at the branches themselves, enjoy them without a green cover, admire the angle and twist of each one.

One winter we had a terrible ice storm. Phone wires snapped and roofs caved in. I woke up on a February morning to see that the Chinese Elm had split almost in two. The weight of frozen water had been too much for it.

The tree surgeon came out in spring and saved it—that is, saved the half that wasn't wounded beyond saving. Parts of the tree were sealed with black gunk, its shape forever altered. A few years passed, and it began to resemble a ghost of its former self.

It never really recovered, and eventually, my parents had it cut down. I was living in Pennsylvania when the phone rang and my parents broke the news. Usually, bad news is about losing people. This time it was about the Chinese Elm, gone for good. I said, "Oh." We went on to talk about jobs, car repairs, and restaurants.

The Chinese Elm is no longer a tree I can hug, but it spreads a warm, green blanket in my mind. I rest in that blanket. I get up and drive to the arboretum where trees dwarf the people instead of industry dwarfing the trees. So many trees! I hug them if so inclined. A grace of leaves welcomes me.

The world is trees, and I am in this world of moths, caterpillars, nesting birds, and bees: creatures, whose lives are as fragile as trees are fragile, letting the shine of trees light their way.

The Big Elm
by Larry Johnson

Most people have special memories about their childhood and early years. Oftentimes, those memories become warmer and a bit more idyllic as the years pass. The specific thoughts and events we recall with fondness in later life may have evolved a bit from what actually took place.

My family moved to a dairy farm in Carver County when I was but a year old; so all of my early memories took place in this rural farming community. Actually, this farm setting was quite normal for Minnesota in the late forties and early fifties. There was always work to be done. I attended a one-room school with about 20 students. Community events were centered around a Swedish Lutheran church and there was no TV. It is truly amazing, as I recall the events of a time not so long ago, that it would be impossible today to recreate the environment in which I grew up.

It is necessary to briefly describe this rural setting in order to demonstrate how a tree can, in fact, be a significant part of so many early and on-going memories. Remember, the world I have just described was very small and self-contained, with virtually no daily exposure to activities to which I could not walk or bike. My world consisted of family, a few neighbor kids, farm animals, the nearby woods, the "crik" and the farm. Oh, yes, this really was no ordinary farm, for right in the center of the farmyard was "The Big Elm."

From the time I learned to talk, to this very day, nobody ever referred to that tree as anything other than The Big Elm. It was no wonder, for it truly was a magnificent specimen. The trunk, at its base, was more than six feet in diameter. It had to be more than seventy feet high and the perfectly proportioned crown was one hundred feet across. The farm driveway circled around its base, the well was on a hill beneath its limbs, and next to the huge trunk was the neighborhood's greatest sandpile, which was replenished with a truckload of sand once a year.

There is no telling how old this tree was. I recall seeing pictures of the farmstead from the thirties and The Big Elm dominated the yard at that time. There is no question, but that whoever first decided to create a farmstead in this particular location did so because they admired the beauty of the tree and could appreciate the shade it would provide. Little did they know the memories which would follow.

As a very young child, I remember the threshing and silo-filling crews gathering in the shade to refresh themselves with the ample supplies of sandwiches, cookies and Kool-Aid provided by my mother. There was always a breeze under The Big Elm. The lunch table always had a red-and-white checkered tablecloth, which occasionally threatened to blow away even though the day had seemed hot and still. The men would often lie down on the grass for a few minutes and someone would invariably say, "That sure is one big tree. If it ever blows down, it will take half of the farmstead with it!" I remember the pride I felt with the knowledge that our farm probably had the biggest tree in the entire world.

As do most large trees, The Big Elm had large root out-croppings, which a small boy could nearly hide in. I recall the warmth of one of those southern-facing crevices between the giant roots on a cold winter's day. Curled up out of the wind on a sunny day, the bark always seemed warm, secure and welcoming. As spring became more evident, I would share this spot with the first brave ants that were attracted by the warmth, and possibly an early sap run.

The sandpile at the base was the center of our daily activities. My brothers and I created elaborate farms with split-rail and string fences, transplanted lambsquarter weeds for trees, broken cement blocks for buildings, and homemade toys to complement the few cast-iron tractors and implements we had received as gifts. The Big Elm formed the western boundary. We piled the sand against The Big Elm to preserve it from gradually moving out into the driveway as a result of summer rains and countless hours of play.

The eastern edge of the sandpile had an embellishment that could only be a reality with a tree such as The Big Elm. It was the grandest and highest swing that I have seen to this day. The first branches of The Big Elm exited the trunk about thirty feet in the air. It was on one of these branches that my father attached two, inch-thick, hay ropes and made a swing seat from a home-sawed, two-by-eight, elm plank. The exhilaration of being pushed by the hired man on that swing could not be matched by any carnival ride. I can still remember the feeling of nearly reaching the overhanging branches, which seemed so distant from the driveway below.

This great swing was also a place of safety and solitude for me as I got older. I always enjoyed heights and became very proficient at rope climbing. It became natural for me to know how far away I was from that swing whenever I was threatened by my brother, who was three years my senior. If I could run to one of those sturdy ropes and climb to more than six feet above ground before he caught me, I would be safe. Once out of reach, I would just wait until he forgot why he was after me or someone else arrived for protection. Other times, I might just climb up onto the great branch to watch the farm animals far below or just wait to surprise the sparrows who might land nearby.

Every spring, I waited for the arrival of the Baltimore Oriole and his mate. This bird absolutely enthralled me with its golden plumage and perfectly clear song. After a long winter of only the drab sparrows and maybe a dimwitted starling, the arrival of the orioles signified that summer would soon be in full swing. I knew that these orioles would build their hanging sock of a nest in The Big Elm, but never once could I find it until after the leaves had fallen. It always seemed that one day in the fall it would just magically appear. I would wonder why I hadn't seen it earlier, even though I had spent many hours lying on my back on the grassy hill, trying to locate it.

When fall came, there was the silo to fill, corn to pick and still the last crop of hay to bring in—all activities centered around the farmyard. The cold north winds would always seem to create a sense of urgency on the farm, just as it does with nature, as birds migrate and squirrels store away food. This same north wind would also blow the yellow and brown leaves from The Big Elm over the entire landscape.

My brothers and I devised a game of catching these leaves, whereby we would select one while it was still high up in the branches. We never knew whether it might fall nearby or whether a gust of wind would carry it over the corncrib or into the cow yard. Even if we were able to position ourselves for the fraction of a second when it was in reach and before it hit the ground, it was still sometimes difficult to catch. I can remember the angry voice of my father when we were engaged in "such foolishness" and had temporarily forgotten our farm duties.

When I turned twenty, I married, and my brother and I purchased the farming business from my father. The Big Elm was still the center of the farmyard, although we had expanded with several larger buildings to the east. The no-longer-used dairy barn burned to the ground in 1973, a neighbor who still harvested corn on the ear moved the corncrib to his farm and a new steel garage was added. The man-made farmstead had changed, but the orioles still arrived on schedule and I still chased an occasional leaf in the fall when I was sure no one was watching. The Big Elm seemed oblivious to the changes, but then it had seen many changes. It always remained the same, except for developing a continuous wet spot on one side of its massive trunk as sap seeped out and slowly leaked to the ground—a disturbing sign of Dutch Elm Disease.

The next year the leaves seemed to let a little more light through than in previous years. But it was the drought year of 1976, and there were more pressing things to be concerned about. There seemed to be less time to enjoy the luxuriant shade, less time to notice the birds or the leaves falling. Our children had graduated from the sandpile much earlier than we had with TV, little league and games from department stores. The swing rope rotted and was never replaced. And, we heard that sometimes, just sometimes, Dutch Elm Disease could be cured. So we tried.

For the next two years, we hired an expert to come out and inject The Big Elm about once each month. I don't think we really thought he could produce a miracle, but after all, this was a family member who had always been there. There was no question; we had to try. The third year, there were only leaves on a couple of branches and they didn't last past late August. I didn't get to catch a one of them.

I remembered the many times I had heard, "If this tree ever blows down...." Now we had to take it down. We hired a professional tree trimmer with spiked shoes, ropes, pulleys, and several chain saws. For a full day he cut and lowered, branch by branch, as my brother and I hauled away The Big Elm. We left the huge trunk with just the shortened stubs of branches as a memorial to more than a century of farm activity.

The branches provided firewood for two fireplaces for the next two years. The oriole family has moved on, replaced by various woodpeckers that still manage to find room and board in The Big Elm. They probably think it couldn't be more perfect.

The Big Elm still stands, but the people who live there now probably don't even have a name for it. It has changed. But then, so has everything else.

Swamp Maple
by Dorothy E. Campbell

after my father's death,
progress and the creation of space
dictated the end of my maple tree
suburban friend,
far too long the only one
that tree held some safety,
held my father's face.

springtime mourning was for me
carved out by its branches
cradled by the sun
it was not enough to cut it down
we somehow made a hole
where its roots firmly wandered
like him, no chance for spring revival
but I took the time to touch its bark,
trace its lower limbs with my farewell hands:
it has eased my pain.

new rooms rise now, insulting angles
stand in its hollow place.

The Father Tree

by Scott Ramsay

Dedicated to my father who was strong, supportive, and loved to share life's stories.

Forty years ago my parents bought a house with a half-acre lot. I was born earlier that year. From pictures, I recall it was quite an open piece of property, except for a string of four beautiful apple trees that marked the boundary between our yard and the neighbors to the east. The first of these trees was right next to the house and it was the biggest. It was on the east side of the house and provided wonderful shade in the summer for my hot, second floor bedroom. The other three trees were evenly spaced about 30 feet apart in an unnaturally straight line toward the back of the property. Since the first tree was the biggest, as a child I assumed it must be the father tree and the other three were its offspring. My father told me they were the remnants of an apple orchard that was there before our house was built. This seemed logical to me, as there were other small orchards around the neighborhood, and the road that our back door neighbors lived on was called Orchard Road.

At a very early age I became fascinated with these trees. The wonderfully fragrant and delicate blossoms in the spring attracted my attention, and that of many different bee species. The flowers would then magically transform into small, green apples. I'll never forget the very first green apple I tasted. Its rather dry, pungent flesh made me wince as it stung my tender tongue. I waited until they turned into larger green apples and then tried them again. The larger ones were certainly more juicy and palatable, but would inevitably cause gastronomic distress. I learned that it was better to wait the seemingly endless four months it took for these fruit gems to ripen, before enjoying this special treat. There was something tantalizing about eating this "wild" fruit that didn't come from a store.

My father had a rule that all apple cores and windfalls had to find their way into the compost pile at the back of the yard. Raking windfalls every fall became my arch nemesis, until I became interested in baseball and thought of a good exercise for my pitching arm. I spent hours lobbing apples across the yard into the compost as fastballs, curves, knuckleballs, changeups and sliders. I don't know if it actually improved my baseball skills, but I was certain that if Harmon Killebrew ever stepped up to the plate, I could ace him with my MacIntosh curve. One day I was picking up a fairly rotted windfall and received a painful surprise as I accidentally squished a yellow jacket that was feeding on the underside of the apple. Another lesson learned, I was much more careful in selecting pitching apples from that time on. I didn't realize at the time what profound lessons those apple trees could teach.

I don't recall how old I was when I first successfully climbed the father tree, but I do recall it was a triumph! The other trees' trunks branched too high up for me to climb, but the father tree's trunk formed a "Y" with two big, inviting, outstretched arms just a few feet above the ground. I managed to shinny up one limb until I could put my knee in that first crotch and then work my way into a standing position. From there, I could reach other branches and raise myself to a perch where several branches intersected and formed a nice, stable seat that I could wedge myself into. From that perch, I gained a grand new perspective on the world. It became a special place where I could take refuge and feel secure. I loved peering across our yard, down the honeysuckle hedge that bordered the lot line, and out into the neighbor's yard from this bird's-eye view. The more time I spent in the canopy of the earth, the more I realized what there was to see. If I sat very still on my perch hugging the branches, I would be joined by visitors who also appreciated the father tree's refuge. Birds and butterflies, beetles and many other insects would light upon the branches just above my head, giving me a sense that I was a part of this greater community of life. The branches supporting me also supported the leaves, which provided welcome shade on a hot summer's day. When the breeze coaxed them to gently rustle, it would lull me to doze. Whenever I was bored or lonesome, the father tree's arms were open, inviting me up to relax and explore. As I clung to the branches, I observed the bark from up close, and a myriad of tiny life-forms became apparent. Ants, spiders and mites had all climbed up the tree from the ground, just as I had. I began to understand what a great provider this tree was, but I really didn't know most of its amazing secrets.

As I grew older, I was able to climb the other trees. But, the father tree was always my favorite, maybe because it was the biggest or because it had that comfortable perch. In time, storms ravaged the other trees, breaking branches and splitting their trunks to the point that they had to be taken down. I was a teenager when my father and I began to cut the damaged trees up to stoke our winter fires. One by one the trees met their demise in descending size order and I knew that it was only a matter of time before the father tree would also bow to time's endless pursuit. I feared for this tree, but it withstood the test of time, perhaps because our house protected it from the ravages of the stormy west wind.

As a teen, I took it upon myself to reforest the yard with silver maple seedlings from the neighbor's father maple tree. I strategically planted each tree in random fashion so they would take the place of the decaying apple trees. The last of the offspring apple trees came down while I was in college, and as my father and I cut it up, I began to realize that my father was also aging. His canopy of hair was thinning and his limbs were weakening, but his heart and spirit were as strong as heartwood. The three offspring apple trees that we loved were gone, but now a towering grove of silver maples was emerging to shade us as we worked in the yard. I'm not so sure my father didn't curse my idea of planting maples as a low maintenance shade tree, for every spring they would drop a deluge of seeds and every fall an ocean of leaves to rake.

Over the years, visiting my parent's house, I took comfort in watching the maples grow to maturity, while the old father apple tree continued to leaf and blossom with its ever-thinning branches. Then one day several years ago, I noticed that half of the father tree was gone. Dad said it had rotted too much and was going to fall; so he cut off the rotted half of the trunk. It bothered me that I had not been present to witness and help out with the reduction of this old favorite tree, perhaps because it was a signal of an era passing.

That tree has been a companion to me my whole life, outliving my dog, my cat and my best high school friend. This past year my

father also succumbed to the relentless pursuit of time and grace-
fully passed from this earth. Amazingly, after forty years of nature's
relentless fury, the now decrepit father apple tree still stands along
the side of the house. Only one arm of the trunk remains, which
curves under the weight of its branches and leaves like an old man
stooping. Its apples are small and full of parasites, yet it continues
to survive and remind me of all the wonderful times I had growing
up under its branches.

Moving the Maple

by Greg Larson

I'd watched it die for years,
the yellow light it shed in autumn
dimming, leaf by leaf;
trunk dropping soft-marrowed branches
in the yard after windstorms
apologetically, as if it could no longer
keep track of everything.

But I didn't witness the final craze of saws,
came home to snow crushed by machines
and pocked by bark broken
when they dragged the brush away.
The trunk lay in sections, scattered
like a campsite of sleepers, heavy backs turned
to the sudden bloom of absence,
a thousand stolen perches opening
like smoke into air.

Still, I couldn't gauge the weight of trees
until I carried this one piecemeal, rolled it,
tore hard hunks of lawn
trundling toward a pyramid
I couldn't fit together:
this wasn't cordwood, not yet,
these thirty rings of seasons pooling outward,
these smaller juts and knots
bearing the heartbeat of rise, spread.

There is no stacking anything
shaped so much like the twist of water
over stones or the fall of light
on the bones of living hands.

The Legend of a Tree
by Frank Finale

Leo's Landscaping is located in a two-story wood frame house that looks as if time passed it by. The house stands on a hill of oak, maple, and pine trees, surrounded by the used car lots, gas stations, and fast-food restaurants of the six-lane Route 37. Its screens are patched but in place, its red paint faded but not yet peeling, and the roof, though intact, has shingles missing. The rain gutters, here and there, overflow with pine needles and leaves.

Leo had called the sign shop where I work, saying, "With all this increased traffic, my house needs a sign that'll catch drivers' attention." So Ray and I drove out to see what we might do for him. Because we picked up speed after the last traffic light, we nearly missed the place. Turning sharply, I navigated the van up the dirt driveway and stopped in a billow of dust, next to a great tree stump that was spiraled with rings. In the yard near the driveway, several pine trees eclipsed the sun, leaving our van in a pool of deep shade.

When we knocked on the weathered screen door, its rusty hinges rattled. Behind us, traffic *whooshed* loudly; inside the house, nothing seemed to move. We knocked even louder before going back to the van; Ray was swearing about the heat and lost time.

As I turned the ignition key, a man in his late 60's opened the screen door. This, presumably, was Leo. I cut the engine as he ambled over to the van. "It's difficult to hear anything on that porch with all those cars *swooshing* by," he said. "Come on, I'll show you what I'm looking for."

Ray and I got out and followed him down to the sign, which was between two four-by-four posts about ten yards from the road. Leo, raising his voice above the methodical hum of traffic, gave us the details of what he wanted on the sign. As we talked, the constant breeze from the cars whipped our hair and ballooned our shirts. Mesmerized by the flow of trucks, cars, vans, and RVs, I said, "I remember when this was a two-lane highway."

Leo laughed. "I've been here forty-five years, and I remember when it was a gravel road."

We stood just outside of the shade of the pines. Ray took notes on how the sign should look. I tried to picture Route 37 as a gravel road, then gave up when the traffic light turned green and, like a dam, released the next rush of cars.

Working my way back into the shade, I said, "You have some magnificent trees here."

"I had a beautiful Norway maple out front by the porch," Leo said. "People used to stop and stare at it. The stump is still there. I couldn't pull it out because of the damned root system. I would've had to tear up the whole front yard and God knows what else."

"What happened?" I asked.

"When they added lanes to Route 37, they took about six feet from my front yard and pruned some of the maple's crown, so that it wouldn't interfere with the telephone wire. About a year later, a telephone worker in a cherry picker comes and saws off large chunks of the maple's branches nearest the highway. He said they were doing it, so they don't have to come back every year to prune. Well, then, I had a one-sided tree. That's not a hell of a good advertisement for a landscaping business, I thought. So me and a couple of my men cut it down—even though it broke my heart to do it. The tree was filled with so much water, we had to wipe the sawblade dry after each cut. It took three men to carry one three-foot piece."

"The following summer," he said, "I couldn't figure out why it was almost twenty-degrees hotter on the porch. Then it dawned on me that the Norway maple had made the difference. That tree was the best damn natural air conditioner around. It kept the noise of the cars down, too."

Ray finished the sketch of the sign and told Leo we'd get back to him. When we returned to the van, I took one last look at the stump. It's great girth and numerous dark and light rings that varied in thickness were a legend of its many years. I pictured the Norway maple as it must have been: a castle of deep-green leaves, symmetrical and lofty with birds, squirrels, and cicadas. On clear days, its hundreds of leaves would be a dazzling green against a radiant sky. When windy, the leaves would rustle and sound like rain, and in fall they'd flush with the season's colors: bright red, orange, and yellow, a wondrous show that made people stop and stare.

With a wave, we left Leo and drove west on Route 37. We passed a new fast-food place with "Grand Opening" buntings draped around its eaves. Farther down the highway, workers in their yellow hard-hats were laying out another strip mall. Under a once branchy sky, black clouds of diesel smoke hung above bulldozers, loaders, and huge dump trucks. Lying in their craters, giant trees bared their amputated roots.

While waiting at a red light, I looked through the heat-wrinkled air above the line of traffic and thought about Shel Silverstein's book, *The Giving Tree*, in which a tree loves a little boy. As the boy grows up, he takes more and more from the tree: shade, leaves, apples, branches for a house, and, in middle age, wood for a boat. When the middle-aged man returns an old man after his many voyages, all that's left of the tree is a stump. The old man sits on it and is, finally, wise enough to appreciate what the tree has given him.

Squinting at the construction site through the waves of exhaust fumes and heat, I thought, for an instant, that I caught the faint outline of children running and playing in the shade. Then Ray called out, "Frank, light's green!" and I drove on.

Clayoquot Is In Our Backyard
by Anneliese Schultz

Trying, as always, to find the good,
I think, 'Perhaps,'
as my heart tears with the ripping bark,
'this could mean seeing more clearly'
new vistas?
ah, seeing a way clear.
More light, by any chance?

I think not—
look away in anguish as she falls—
a clear view now of distant neighbors' dormers,
T.V. antennas,
empty sky.
Vision stopped at the gaping orange mouth
Fuzzy city street illumination of
telephone wire and electric air.

Thinking does not bring her back—
godly and embracing pine, she who watched over
the children of these woods, then pastures,
dirt, then black-paved streets for generations;
home to uncountable cycles of creatures,
to sun and shade,
to my first peaceful gaze of morning,
and the heady boughs of Christmas—

These my son and I gather now in July,
crying as the bulldozer spins above us,
and thinking,
'How will we keep your branches
ever green?'

Tribute to a Friend Who Died Fighting
by Judy Hoffman

This is a story for a dear friend. He lived in the area of town my husband and I call "the war zone," around the corner of Holcomb Bridge Road and U.S. Highway 19, in Roswell, Georgia. For a while, he had lots of friends around him and wasn't very noticeable. As time passed, more and more of his companions were struck down until there were only two left. Since one was smaller, I couldn't help but feel she was his mate, and that somehow they managed together to survive.

I used to see them standing proudly on top of the hill, as I drove along Holcomb Bridge Road, looking absolutely magnificent as they contemptuously ignored the chaos and ugliness below them. I, too, tried not to look at all that bare ground and tackiness, concentrating on them and their beauty for as long as I could, before I had to turn my eyes once again to six lanes of ugly black asphalt.

Then, one day in early summer, my friend's mate was cut and carried away and only he was left: one old, tall, stately tree—standing alone—a single monument to all the beauty that once was there.

As days passed, I began to notice that he didn't look as handsome as he used to. His bark was covered with dust, a pile of bricks sat on his roots, his limbs and leaves looked sad and droopy. At first, I passed this off as shock from the construction going on around him and from a lack of rain. But later, after the removal of the bricks and the arrival of rain, he still looked terrible. It was then I realized he was dying; his grief was too great to bear.

As I would drive by, I would often send him words of encouragement, hoping against hope that somehow he would rally and live. And he did. Like the majestic old warrior that he was, he began to stand straight again. Somehow, the sight of him on the horizon made me feel more hopeful about things in general. That's when he went from being my good friend to being my special friend.

Last weekend my husband and I were driving by, talking and laughing and having a very pleasant time, when suddenly I saw him. He was lying on his side chopped up in big pieces, his stump all scarred and battered. My tree was dead.

I started to cry. I cried all the way home with my husband patting my hand and muttering to himself about the stupidity of chopping down one lone tree that wasn't bothering anybody.

At last, I managed to stop crying, and tried to tell myself that perhaps my tree will fill someone's fireplace with his wood. At least he could go out in a blaze of glory. That comforted me a bit. But later, as I lay in bed, I started to cry again. The next day I couldn't seem to stop crying. I couldn't figure out why all this excess emotion over one tree.

Finally, I realized the loss of this tree was more than the loss of something beautiful. It was the loss of what it symbolized that was causing all my heartache. For to me, this tree stood for all the fighters in this world—and there are many—who against insurmountable odds just won't give up.

I see them all the time. Little children running in a race with big children, knowing full well they can't possibly win. Yet they give it all they've got, their faces flushing and lungs bursting as they collapse in defeat at the finish line.

Adults somehow managing to go through their days, coping, handling responsibilities and making decisions. At the same time their emotional worlds are caving in on them, with the termination of a job, the disappointment in a child or the loss of a loved one.

And my husband, who sees both children and adults in the biggest battle of all—the battle to live. At the hospital, he sees very sick people fighting, fighting hard to make it. And when one of them doesn't, it tears him apart.

So that's why I mourn the loss of my tree. He went down, but he went down fighting. I understand that. Still, I know that there will be a permanent scar on the landscape because he's gone, and there will also be a permanent scar on my heart.

Touched By a Tree
by Mahria Potter

I have always been touched by trees. As a young woman living on a tree-filled island in the inland sea of Puget Sound, I rode my bike the three miles to and from high school. Gliding by the ravine filled with big-leaf maples, wild red alder and cedar trees, I was drawn to stop and visit them many times.

Pulling my bike off the road, I meandered through, feeling the rough bark of the Douglas fir and the softness of the maple mamas. They beckoned me to come and sit in the fern and leaf debris and smell the mushroom-laden earth.

To know our forests, one must do just that. Know them. The deep greens of sword fern and moss and salal stand steady and proud beneath the majestic and commanding evergreens. As the sunlight filters through, it doesn't matter whether it shines or not. When you are engulfed in green, a gray sky is as welcome as a blue one.

Looking around and above, the branches called in patterns of a language spoken and understood by a wood's dweller. Here the evergreens hang, mellow, satisfied in their place. The more wildly expressive deciduous, however, call out: "I am here, I am here!"

It was on one meander that I found the most enchanting triple-trunked red alder. At the time, I called it birch and maybe it was. Its base was not so thick—maybe 36 inches around—yet immediately branching into three sweet selves. I felt the spirit was large and full and yearned to feel three times the canopy, rather than just one perspective.

Every couple of days, I visited my triple birch. I sang her songs of love and of the difficulty of having just lost my lover to college. She witnessed my tears and I hugged her, sensing her understanding. As I entered the ravine, my song and dance would erupt upon sighting her and I would encircle her with my instinctual dance of life and love.

Then I would speak of this and that, knowing full well she was listening. She knew me and I knew her. I visited her over the summer and into my next year. Then, the island began exploding and people began to build and build.

One day, in pulling my bicycle off the road and into the safety I had known, I saw her. Her trunks stood a perfect 18 feet off the ground debodied so perfectly. Beside the beautiful triple stump stood a triangle of six beautiful logs neatly stacked. For me, the death was complete. I could not accept it, though now I feel life is always changing and growing. The gifts of her life and her death are always there. But, at the time, I felt completely betrayed by the human race. How could they not see? I fell to the ground and screamed my pain and anguish. I traced her body with my fingers feeling her spirit and yet not. I knew she was gone. I felt totally alone, forced into abandonment by some greedy woodcutter.

Alone, and missing her terribly, I went back two more times to visit and just make sure. It was hard to accept. She was the first tree I had ever truly loved and felt its love back. Not since then have I had such luxury of privacy and trust. I will never, ever forget her.

The Secret of the Seed
by Dennis Saleh

Once, all the different parts
of a tree were in a terrible
argument over who had claim
to own what. The root said,
it was oldest, and so claimed
all the ground. The trunk said,
it was broadest, and thus,
claimed most of the light. The
fruit said it was the sweetest
part, and thereby entitled
to man's favor. The wood
explained, without it, there
would be no boats, so the
lumber of the tree wished all
the seas. The leaves said
they had to reach up into the
air highest, so they wanted
the sky. All of this time, the
seed had remained quiet,
listening to the others, making
no comment, being youngest.
Finally, after each had spoken,
the seed spoke at last, saying,
"I ask for nothing. I will
take the future."

Afterword

The soul of a tree is difficult to define, as is the soul of a human being. But I am deeply convinced that it was the soul of a maple tree in Cades Cove that spoke comforting words to me in 1971, and in 1996 implanted within my consciousness the seed for this anthology.

I have been truly blessed with meaningful connections throughout the creation of this volume of stories and poems. When I initially placed an ad for submissions in the *Poets and Writers Journal* in late 1997, to my amazement and delight, I was over-whelmed with responses. For several months, I excitedly raced home from work to read the day's collection and cherish the fact that many authors included personal notes of gratitude for the opportunity to tell of their special tree. As a result of this project, I have met dedicated people whose passion is an unwavering commitment to the healing of our environment. I have been touched by the creations of superbly talented writers, poets, storytellers and photographers. And as I have shared with others my enthusiasm concerning this book, I have been warmed by their smiles of identification, as well as by their gaze of reconnection with cherished memories.

In Paulo Coelho's gem, *The Alchemist*, the primary character, Santiago, sets forth upon a journey of personal and spiritual growth and enlightenment. Through a series of confluential events, he discovers three of life's core lessons: to pay attention to signs, to listen to one's heart, and to follow one's dreams. The journey of my life has been forever altered and immeasurably enriched through an encounter with a maple tree, an encounter which has taught me to pay attention to my signs, to listen to my heart, and to follow my dreams.

Warren D. Jacob

Contributors

CYNTHIA A. ARNETT is a true country girl and reluctant city dweller with a condo garden, but currently no Mulberry trees. Having been in the medical field for over 25 years as a medical transcriptionist, her spare time is spent enjoying walks, reading, playing piano, and watching college basketball.

GEORGE BAGGETT is a native Kansas City, Missourian, and has worked in the environmental field since 1973. As a teenager, George met Chief Justice William O. Douglas on a canoe trip on the Buffalo River in Arkansas. After hearing Justice Douglas talk around the campfire, and with the influence of his conservation-minded father, George has since considered environmental issues to be important. He currently designs waste water plants.

J. P. DANCING BEAR is of Chippewa and Swedish ancestry. His poems have been published in hundreds of journals, magazines and anthologies, including *New York Quarterly, Zuzu's Petals Quarterly, Slipstream, Pearl, Conspire, Eclectica, Montserrat Review,* and *Rio Grande Review.* He authored four chapbooks: *From a Reconstructed Dream, Disjointed Constellations, Prospero in Therapy* and *Atlas.*

RICHARD BEBAN lives in Venice, CA, where he finds the magnolia tree (and its inhabitants) outside his window a constant source of poetic inspiration. A long-time environmental activist, he writes grant applications and proposals for environmental organizations like Los Angeles-based *TreePeople.* A poet since 1994, he has been published in eight national anthologies and many magazines.

SHANTI BENOIT (formerly Finerty) graduated in Art from Oberlin College and now lives on forest land near the coastal village of Mendocino, CA. Her writings, *Cabin Fever, Million Dollar Meadow* and *High Ground,* have appeared in literary publications. Her subject matter suggests a grove of trees to enclose and protect, holding us to what is important, vital, and inspiring in life.

SUSANA BOUQUET-CHESTER lived, as a child, in Mexico, Cuba and Brazil. She studied psychology at Columbia University. After some years as a professor and Peace Corps researcher, she went to Woodstock, NY, and entered private practice, writing in her spare time. Upon retiring, she devoted herself to writing. She has published extensively in both professional and popular magazines. "The Lesson of the Kapok Tree" appeared in *St. Petersburg Times,* 1998.

GRACE BUTCHER retired in 1993 (emeritus) from twenty-five years of teaching English and twelve years of coaching the running program at the Kent State University Geauga Campus. Her poetry has appeared in *Poetry, The Literary Review, Louisville Review, Passages North, Tar River Poetry, Poetry East, Nimrod* and in numerous anthologies. She was named Ohio Poet of the Year in 1992 for *Child, House, World,* Hiram Poetry Review. "Learning from Trees" appeared in *Poetry,* April, 1991.

DOROTHY E. CAMPBELL lives in Bedford Village, New York, with two daughters, an assortment of dogs and cats, and more than 40 trees. She is currently pursuing a Master of Arts in Writing at Manhattanville College and works in the South Bronx.

VIVINA CIOLLI has published in *Poets On, Long Island Quarterly, Sistersong, Negative Capability, The Maryland Poetry Review.* Her chapbook *Bitter Larder* won the June, 1994, New Spirit Press Chapbook Competition and *Consolation of Dreams* won the Talent House Press Competition in 2001.

MICHAEL COLLINS is a math teacher at Babylon High School, Long Island, NY. The first writing he ever did was in college for a class on writing short stories. A girlfriend read what he was writing and asked him if he would ever write anything about her. The title of his story, *A Maple*, is an anagram of her name.

CLARA COURTEAU is a retired nursing home staffing coordinator. Her favorite hobby/pastime is visiting wildlife areas in search of birds, wildflowers, and other wild things. She is on the board of directors of the Springbrook Nature Center Foundation in Fridley, MN, and works with the birdbanding program.

CHUCK DOBBS is a storyteller who has written down several of the stories he tells. He and the "love of his life," Dahleen, a talented photographer, live in Nevada.

WALTER ENLOE is a professor of education and liberal arts at Hamline University in St.Paul, MN. For eighteen years he taught K-12 at the Paideia School in Atlanta and K-9 as the Teacher Principal of Hiroshima International School. His most recent books are co-authored, *Learning Circles* and *Encounters with Hiroshima.*

LISA FAY uses nature in her paintings, photographs and poems. She attends workshops and visits different locations to gain new ideas. Trees are in her blood as her father owned a tree and landscape company when she was young. "Backyard Tree" first appeared in *The Fenway News.*

FRANK FINALE has more than 270 poems and essays published in more than a hundred books, journals and magazines. In 1996, he co-edited, with Rich Youmans, *Under A Gull's Wing*, the critically acclaimed anthology of poems and photographs about the Jersey Shore. "Legend of a Tree" first appeared in *COAST Magazine,*1989, and is included in *Shore Stories,* 1998, and in *To The Shore Once More,*1999.

CAROL FJELD is a 50-something mother of two great 20-something kids. She recently migrated to Wyoming's incredibleness as an innkeeper of a small old bed & breakfast in Saratoga. She is completing an English-Creative Writing degree at Colorado University. Her poems have been in published in *Writer's Journal, Sierra Nevada College Review* and *Promise Magazine..*

DOROTHY K. FLETCHER has been a language arts teacher in the Duval County School System for the past 26 years. She has had over 60 poems published in various literary journals. Her work has appeared most recently in *The Main Street Rag, Messages From the Heart,* and *The Artful Mind.* She has written a children's book, *The Week of Dream Horses.*

C. B. FOLLETT'S poems have appeared in *Peregrine, The Cumberland Review, The Taos Review, South Coast Poetry Review,* and *Psychological Perspectives.* She has been nominated for five Pushcart Prizes and has been the recipient of numerous Honorable Mentions, including the 1999 National Poetry Book Award from Salmon Run Press.

ROBERT C. FUENTES states, "I was born onto a planet where I have learned that the hands of mother nature can gently mold us each day in ways we may never realize...until we finally stop to look and rediscover who we are."

LARRY R. GRANGER is a lifelong resident of Minnesota. He currently serves as a diversified consultant to communities and organizations in the area of historical interpretation, school and community partnerships and community design. His past work has included assisting citizens of Southwestern Minnesota to develop the first Ecology Bus in North America.

JILL HAMMER works at Ma'yan: The Jewish Women's Project at the JCC in Manhattan. She was ordained as a rabbi by the Jewish Theological Seminary in 2001, and holds a Ph.D. in social psychology from the University of Connecticut. She is a poet and author whose first book is entitled, *Sisters at Sinai: New Tales of Biblical Women.*

JOHANNA HERRICK has for over thirty years worked as an English teacher, librarian and teacher trainer. Her passion for writing poetry is part of a broader quest for the spiritual interconnectedness of all things. She has published numerous poems in small literary journals, including *Chaminade Literary Review, Waterways, Poets' Edge, Night Roses,* and *Poets' Corner.*

JACKIE LEE HOFER has been in the book trade for thirty years as an author and book publisher. His latest book is *One Harmonic Whole: The Song of the Universe.*

JUDY HOFFMAN is a freelance writer and has been a columnist for the Roswell-Alpharetta Neighbor and the Forsyth County News. She lives with her husband and two dogs among "the few remaining trees" in Alpharetta, GA. She is proud that she saved a 100-year-old oak tree in her neighborhood by threatening to expose the developer in her newspaper column. "Tribute to a Friend Who Died Fighting" appeared in *Roswell/Alpharetta Neighbor* newspaper.

MARION I. HOWE was born on a farm near Goodhue, MN, in 1915. She studied surgical nursing under Dr. Charlie Mayo and graduated in 1939. Marion had a lifetime interest in organic farming (her father farmed organically with horses until his death in 1956). Marion died in 1999.
(Thank you to her son, Roy Howe, for the poem and the bio - Eds)

LARRY JOHNSON grew up on a grain and turkey farm in Carver County, MN, and operated the farm for 25 years until founding his consulting business in 1987. In 1975 he built a house on the corner of a 17-acre pasture. His interest in nature and the environment led him to reforest the pasture with more than 8,000 trees. He continues to live in a corner of his forest with his wife, Sandy. Their three grown children all live within a ten mile drive.

MARTY KRAFT is an environmental educator who works with Heartland All Species Project in Kansas City, MO. He states, "I'm in a love relationship with nature. She is a conscious, ever-changing mystery in which I find the Presence. That Presence includes me. It must be the breath or the shelter of God."

GREG LARSON earned his M.A. in creative writing at Iowa State University and is currently on the editorial staff at Milkweed Editions in Minneapolis. His work has appeared in *Controlled Burn* and *Defined Providence*.

JEAN LENGWIN lives on a small ranch near Grants Pass in Southern Oregon. Her home is nestled in a stand of tall, stately fir trees. A generous number of trees native to the area are scattered throughout the property—oak, maple, cedar, madrona, wild pear and plum. She began writing nonfiction when her favorite pen-friend passed away and Jean found herself frustrated with bottled-up words. Her works have appeared in local newspapers, anthologies and magazines.

KATHLEEN LOHR is a Los Angeles screenwriter, filmmaker and poet. Her script/project, *Brainiacs*, premiered on the Disney Channel in February, 2001. Kathleen has had films with HBO, Miramax and Blockbuster, and last year produced *Pandamania*, a co-production with the People's Republic of China from her original screenplay. Kathleen's poetry has appeared in *Red Dancefloor Press*, *Shelia-na-gig*, *51%* and *Chiron Review*.

PEG LOPATA is a freelance writer and painter in New Hampshire. She is a contributing writer for Seacoast Newspapers, Portsmouth, NH. Her work has appeared in *Adoptive Families*, *Mothering*, *Plain* and numerous other magazines.

ROBIN LOPEZ LYSNE is the author of *Dancing Up the Moon* and *Living a Sacred Life*. Her poems have appeared in *Besides the Sleeping Maiden*, *Emerald Street Poets Review* and *Korone*. She leads workshops and presentations across the country, often incorporating her poetry. She lives among the redwoods in CA.

LAURA C. MARTIN is native to Atlanta and has worked as a freelance writer specializing in nature, gardening and crafts for over 20 years. She has published 17 books, including *Folklore of Trees and Shrubs,* as well as many articles in both local and national periodicals. She serves as garden editor for *Atlanta Homes and Lifestyles* magazine and is a regular contributor to *Better Homes and Gardens Special Interest Publications.*

LOUIS MARTINELLI is a poet, playwright and essayist. He is the author of *I Saw a Light That Was a River Flowing* and *Connecting Generations Through Storytelling*. He has received the Iowa Arts Council's Outstanding Achievement Award for his play, *Take My Hand*. His lifelong interest in connecting health, caregiving and ecology led him to write *Carrying Water to Trees*.

ROCHELLE MASS moved from Canada with her husband and daughters to a kibbutz in the Jezre'el Valley in Israel where she lived for almost 30 years. She has participated in the Steven Spielberg Visual History Foundation as an interviewer of Holocaust survivors, and is the editor of *Kibbutz Trends*. Published widely in anthologies and journals both in Israel and abroad, she has won a number of awards. In 2001, her poetry was published in *Aftertaste* and *Where's My Home*. She has been nominated for the 2002 27th Annual *Pushcart Poetry Prize*.

MARIAN MILLS-GODFREY, a born and bred Kansas Jayhawker, is a world traveler and published writer who revels in retirement following a counseling career with middle school students. She grew up on a 1000 acre wheat farm near the geographical center of the United States. She enjoys writing poems, essays, articles or nostalgic stories that emerge from those rich roots. "Branches of Life" appeared in *Handprint in the Woods* by Whispering Prairie Press, 1997.

JENNY MICHELLE NADANER grew up in British Columbia and California. The inspiration for her poem came from hiking trips from San Francisco Bay to the Pacific Ocean and other moments of meditation on the magnificent redwoods and pine trees of Northern California. She counts Marquez and his magical realism as a major influence on her writing.

PAIDEIA SCHOOL STUDENTS "Most children have experienced a tree story. It may involve a tree they have climbed and conquered...or one hidden behind in fantasy adventures. Perhaps the children have enjoyed the sweet fruits of the tree...or simply the pleasure of throwing those fruits at a tempting target. A few have been frightened by the power and fragility of these seeming giants. Some children have lost their trees to storms or saws or moves to new homes, but the trees live on in imaginations and memories. Our writing assignment, inspired by Shel Silverstein's, *The Giving Tree*, taps the strong emotions and images associated with the trees of childhood." The children who wrote these stories were 5th and 6th graders in Lina Wessels and Brian Eames' class at the Paideia School, an independent school in Atlanta, GA. (Bio written by Lina Wessels - Thanks - Eds)

KENNETH POBO teaches English at Widener University and received his Ph.D. in English from the University of Wisconsin at Milwaukee. His poems and stories have appeared in *The Philadelphia Inquirer* magazine, *Colorado Review, Nimrod, Atlanta Review, Orbis, Wascana Review, Indiana Review* and elsewhere. His books include *Cicadas in the Apple Tree* and *Ordering: A Season in My Garden*.

MAHRIA POTTER is a proud Washingtonian who balances storytelling, delivery driving, environmental education in local clubs through songwriting and performing, and most importantly of all, parenting two beautiful children. Mahria transmits her passion in words and songs that awaken the "lover" of the earth in each of us. This is her life's work.

SCOTT RAMSAY is a professional Interpretive Naturalist and outdoor enthusiast. He enjoys hiking, fishing, hunting, camping, cycling and canoeing with his lovely wife, Dana. Scott's writings are based on his experiences growing up in Minnetonka, MN. His story is in memory of his father, Dr. George Alan Ramsay.

DAVID RAY'S books include *The Tramp's Cup, The Touched Life, Sam's Book, Kangaroo Paws, Wool Highways,* and *The Maharani's New Wall,* as well as *Fathers,* an anthology co-edited with his wife, Judy. Two of his titles have won the William Carlos Williams Award from The Poetry Society of America, and two have been nominated for a Pulitzer Prize. His most recent book, *Demons in The Diner,* won the Richard J. Snyder Memorial Award.

MARY REITER has lived in Richfield, MN, on a wooded park for 61 years. She is a political activist and environmentalist.

RICHARD RISEMBERG was born in Argentina and raised in Los Angeles from the age of three. He is a vegetarian, hiker, cyclist and conservationist. As a writer and photographer, he has been published in a number of collections. He is presently editing *Living Room,* a web magazine and a forum on Urban Ecology.

DENNIS SALEH is the author of five books of poetry, the most recent of which, *This Is Not Surrealism,* won the first chapbook competition from Willamette River

Books. His poetry, prose and artwork appear widely, in such magazines as *ArtLife*, *Artword Quarterly*, *Bitter Oleander*, *Black Dirt*, *Happy*, *Nedge*, *Poetry Conspiracy*, *Pearl*, *Prairie Schooner*, *Psychological Perspectives* and *Social Anarchism*. His poems also appear in two anthologies, *How Much Earth* and *The Geography of Home*. "The Secret of the Seed" appeared in *Shoofly Magazine*.

FOREST SHOMER is a native-plant seedsman residing in Port Townsend, WA.

ANNELIESE SCHULTZ'S short story, *27 Years*, was a finalist in both the 1997 Writers' Union of Canada Short Prose Competition and the 1998 Toronto Star Short Story Contest. She received an honorable mention in the 1998 Writer's Digest Competition children's fiction category for her book, *Snow Soup*, and was a finalist in the 1999 Heekin Group Foundation Writing Fellowships Program. "Clayoquot Is In Our Backyard" appeared in *Witness to the Wilderness*, 1994

LAURA SNYDER is a poet, botanical illustrator and naturalist. Her writing has appeared in *Grrr: A Collection of Poems About Bears*, *Earth's Daughters*, *Least Loved Beasts of the Really Wild West* and in three online magazines, *Switched on Gutenberg*, *The Horsethief's Journal* and *The Green Tricycle*. "Tree, Why Do You Bind Me" appeared in *Island Independent*, August, 1995, and in *Cutting Trees: An Island Independent Forum, Part 1*, August 17-30, 1995, Whidbey Island, WA.

MICHAEL STEPHANS is a professional musician with many recordings, TV and film, as well as extensive worldwide live performances. He is on the faculty at Pasadena City College. He is the author of *Bright Size Life*, *Mythematics* and *The Color of Stones*. His literary awards include Poet of the Year (Inscape Magazine), Grand Prize (Conejo Valley Poetry Festival), Fiction Prize (Red Dancefloor Press) and Pushcart Prize Nominee (Verve Magazine).

NICOLE S. URDANG is a writer and holistic psychotherapist in Buffalo, NY. She has had essays, short stories and poems published in *The New York Times*, *Libido*, *Words on Paper*, *FYI*, *Psychopoetica* (UK), *The Buffalo News*, *Radiance*, *Buffalo Spree*, *Metropolis*, *Zeitgeist*, *Hard Choices*, *Lovers & Liars*, *A Sense of Place*, *The Best Contemporary Women's Humor* and *Glibquips*. Nicole is also a frequent contributor to WBFO, the local NPR affiliate.

CLAUDIA VAN GERVEN resides in Boulder, CO, where she teaches writing. Her work has appeared in numerous magazines, including *Prairie Schooner*, *Calyx* and *The Lullwater Review*. Her work has been widely anthologized, with *I Am Becoming the Woman I've Wanted*, winning the 1997 Angel Fish Press contest. Her manuscript, *The Spirit String*, was a finalist in the 1998 Backwaters Press Prize.

TERESA W. WOLFE is an herbalist with a degree in Food Science and Nutrition. She has over 20 years teaching experience in the areas of biological sciences, nutrition, herbalism and environmental education. She was a regular columnist for *Twin Cities Wellness* magazine in Minneapolis/St. Paul, MN. Teresa practices what she refers to as "Eco-Herbalism," which focuses on the restoration of balance to humanity and the planet.

Editors and Photographer

WARREN D. JACOBS is a psychiatrist/psychotherapist in private practice in Atlanta, GA. His most recent therapeutic interests include working with hospice and issues of dying, grief and bereavement. In Japan, it is said, a person may define one's identity based upon the deep expression of the soul, and not necessarily by one's daily occupation. In that same manner, Warren's soul identity is that of a composer of music and storyteller. He creates Jewish choral and folk music using material from the Hebrew prayer book and Bible. His stories include the telling of Hasidic parables, Jewish folktales, and personal experiences. He has told stories in many venues in the Atlanta area, including the Carter Center and the 1999 Arbor Day Atlanta celebration. In 1992, he produced a tape of his music entitled, *Shirei Nafshi - Songs of My Soul*. Warren has also written poetry, several pieces of which have been published in professional journals. This anthology is his first book

KAREN I. SHRAGG is the director of Wood Lake Nature Center in Richfield, MN. Karen lectures on environmental lifestyles at colleges, grade schools and regional and national professional naturalists' associations. She was a founding member of the Minnesota Earth Day network and co-chaired the 1995 25th anniversary celebration of Earth Day for Minnesota. Karen has led eco-tours to Costa Rica and lectures on rain forest issues. Under the name, "Shanberg," she has co-authored three books, including *Plantworks, Start Mushrooming* and *Nature Smart*. She received the Excellence in Interpretation award from the National Association for Environmental Interpretation for Plantworks. Karen received an award form the Midwest Independent Publishers' Associaton for "Best How-To Book" for *Start Mushrooming*. She is the author of the children's book, *A Solstice Tree for Jenny*, and she co-authored the picture book, *Nature's Yucky*.

CAROL WEEKS has been a photographer since 1982. Her love of nature led her to pursue her first career as a professional naturalist and educator, and to her present calling as a photographer. She enjoys the challenge of capturing nature's beauty with the camera. Carol's work has won several major awards and has appeared in showcase and juried exhibitions, as well as fine art festivals around the country. Hand-printed, limited editions of the color cover photo may be ordered by contacting Carol at *carolweeks@citcom.net* or see the web site *www.nfrog.com* for more information.

Publisher and Editors' Gratitude To Trees

We realize that if it weren't for trees, this book would never be. So we give thanks to the trees for all they provide us and for how important they are in our lives. May this book show people the specialness of trees and that the supply of trees is not unlimited.

The text of this book has been printed on recycled, acid-free paper using environmentally friendly soy-based ink.

If you have a tree story or poem you would like to submit for a follow-on publication to *Tree Stories*, please send it to:

Tree Stories
SunShine Press Publications
P. O. Box 333
Hygiene, CO 80533-0333

As the poet said, "only God can make a tree," probably because it's so hard to get the bark on.
—*Woody Allen*

Dedications

Warren:

> For "The Wedding Tree" who gave life to the idea for this book and for Judie, Elana and Rebecca, who give life to me.

Karen:

> For Dick Powell, the real writer in our family, who would've truly enjoyed this collection.

Acknowledgments

Karen and I would like to profusely thank all of those who shared their wonderful stories and poems with us. By sharing your deeply felt tales you have touched our lives, and now these amazing stories have an opportunity to touch many others. Perhaps this collection will help give even more people permission to share their special relationships with trees.

In addition, I wish to include my heartfelt thanks to the following people, all of whom have blessed my life wih their contribution to the actualization of this anthology.

I am deeply grateful to Jackie and Gretchen Hofer of SunShine Press Publications, who have been generous with their time and expertise and who have been consistently available, constructive, creative, attentive and encouraging. Their warmth, integrity and friendship have made this process a most enjoyable experience. Every writer should have publishers like Jackie and Gretchen.

Thanks to Carol Weeks for her magnificent photograph of "my" maple tree in full fall glory and to Dave Goldman whose skills as a printer brought her image to life.

I am indebted to Rochelle Mass for her critiques and insights, but more importantly, for her listening ear and warm friendship.

Thanks to Lou Martinelli who also reviewed my story and offered several helpful suggestions.

A word of gratitude to my men's group—Gerald Drose, Martin Fleet, Warren Kaplan, Rick Rasche and Jim Struve—for sharing their excitement, companionship and support, and, to Rick and Jim, who suggested I contact Lina Wessels' and Brian Eames' 6th grade class at Paideia School. Thanks to Lina and Brian for allowing me to meet their students and publish their stories, and to Nancy Johnson for her assistance.

Thanks to my peer group—Barbara McNew, Dan Mermin, Frank Ostrowski, Carolyn Rasche and Janet Tyler—who, for the many years we have met, have always challenged me and nurtured me along my journey.

I wish to extend my appreciation to Stuart Finestone for his guidance during some of the rough spots; to Karen Quidgley for her suggestions, enthusiasm and warm smile; to Elaine Friedman for her soulful spirit; to Carrell Dammann, colleague and mentor, for her deep wisdom and supportive presence; a special thanks to Janis Kleinberger for her gentle friendship and belief in the importance of this book; to Diane and Alan Evans for their invaluable friendship and for Alan's tireless efforts in helping me to promote this book; and to Jo and Louis Pichulik for their love and abiding closeness.

And where would I be without the constant love of my family—to my parents, Betty and Joseph Jacobs, whose strength and perseverance have truly been an inspiration and a model for living; to my brother, Howard, and his wife, Judy, who have been so helpful with media connections; to my daughter, Elana (whose name is Hebrew and means "oak tree"), who introduced me to Karen and of whom I am proud as she works to perform Tikkun Olam (repair of the world); to my daughter, Rebecca, who found Carol's photo of "my" tree at a craft fair in Atlanta and whose infectious smile lights my heart; and to my wife, Judie, an incredibly talented ceramic artist, sculptor, painter and teacher, whose love, acceptance, honesty, integrity and directness help me stay on the correct path.

—Warren David Jacobs, Atlanta, GA